Design

Below: Four-fifths of the Type VII U-boats built, their hull numbers emblazoned in distinctively styled white numerals on the conning towers and—as can just be seen at the foot of the photograph—on bow plaques. The ten vessels of this flotilla are often referred to as 'Type VIIA' U-boats in order to distinguish them from the many derivative designs that followed.

IN common with all naval construction of World War II, the design heritage of German warships and combat craft can be traced directly to the experience garnered during the first great conflict some twenty-five years earlier. Unlike the rest of the world's navies, however, the overbearing influence of the inter-war years was not the Washington Treaty of 1922 but rather the Treaty of Versailles of 1919, the harsh terms of which not only bred resentment within the German naval heirarchy but also brought about a clandestine industry determined to keep alive the technical expertise built up during 1914–18.

In March 1935 the British National Government published a White Paper entitled *Statement Relating to Defence*, which in effect discarded the terms of Versailles and recognised the right of Germany to rearm; three months later Ramsay MacDonald's ministers signed the Anglo-German Naval Treaty, one of the most important provisions of which was that permitting Germany to build U-boats once more, nominally up to a strength of 45 per cent of the British submarine fleet but perhaps, 'in case of danger [from Russia]', to par—in effect, a blank cheque.

This treaty, castigated by some writers as signalling the end of all hopes of peace with Adolf Hitler, in fact did little more than recognise officially what was taking place and inevitably would continue to take place—the build-up of the German military machine. What it did not acknowledge, nor probably did it tacitly understand, were the overbearing single-mindedness of the German leadership to nullify what were construed as the injustices and indignities of the Treaty of Versailles and Hitler's arrogant determination to achieve unparalleled German hegemony.

LATENT TECHNOLOGY

The Germans' desire to continue the development of their U-boat fleet was expressed not long after the imposition of the ban on the construction of further submarines that was enshrined within the terms of the Treaty of Versailles (Article 19) when, in 1921, the Argentine Navy invited three former U-boat technical experts to provide assistance in the construction of a new class of submarines. This opportunity was seized eagerly, and within a year, with Reichsmarine backing, a front organisation, N. V. Ingenieurskaantor voor Scheepsbouw (IvS) was established in The Hague.

In the event, this collaborative project came to naught, as did a similar approach made at around the same time by the Italian Navy and another, in 1924, by the Spanish. IvS languished for some months, until in 1926 it became involved in the design and construction of two boats being built for the Turkish Navy: based on the German Type UB III of World War I, these vessels offered the opportunity to IvS of gaining first-hand knowledge of their performance in trials—a vital experience denied to the Germans since the end of the war. Then, following some energetic lobbying, came a firm order for three minelaying submarines for Finland. Based on the Type UC III, these were launched from 1930 and were followed by a 250/300-ton boat (*Vesikko*) which served as the prototype for the German Type II U-boat of World War II. A revival of interest by Spain led to the construction, with considerable German technical assistance, of a small (760/960-ton) submarine which, launched in 1932, eventually had to be transferred to Turkey (and renamed *Gur*); her design was utilised as the basis for the German Type IA and, through it, the Type VII.

'MOTORENVERSUCHSBOOTE'

By this time plans for a resuscitated German submarine arm were well in hand, and in the autumn of 1932 they received official blessing with the decision to set up the cagily termed Motorenversuchsboot (Experimental Motor Boat) division within the Navy, with the objective of having sixteen new U-boats in commission by 1938. Four were to be based on the Spanish-built *Gur* and the remaining twelve—for coastal duties—on the small Finnish *Vesikko*. The two types were designated, respectively, MVB I and MVB II, and the designs evolved over the following months pending official sanction to convert plans into hardware. Meanwhile the Unterseebootsabwehrschule (U-Boat Defence School) was established for the purpose of training future German submariners

The official sanction to proceed with the construction programme came early in 1935. Three companies were involved: the larger of the two types (I) would be built by Deschimag A. G. Weser at

Above: *U 32* at the time of the Spanish Civil War, and wearing neutrality stripes down the conning tower (red forward, white and black). The arrangement of drainage holes along the hull of the Type VII was radically modified in later sub-types, and a further distinguishing feature was of course the above-water torpedo tube at the stern. Screening appears to have been draped here and there over the deck guard rail in this photograph. The initial gun armament layout of single 8.8cm forward and single 20mm on the main deck aft is shown here also.

Left: Karl Dönitz, who did much to help establish the U-Boat Service and was responsible for its direction during World War II. It was his drive and enthusiasm—in the face of bitter opposition at first from the 'big-gun' proponents within the Kriegsmarine—that turned the Atlantic Ocean into such a desperate battleground. He is seen here with 'Parsifal' Wohlfarth (*U 556*), who has just received the Iron Cross.

COURTESY LAWRENCE PATERSON

Above: The Type VII *U 36*. This boat was an early war loss, blown to smithereens in the north-eastern North Sea after being torpedoed by HM Submarine *Salmon* in December 1939.

Bremen and the smaller (II)—now appearing as two distinct sub-types, A and B—at Kiel, by Germaniawerft and Deutsche Werke.

TYPE VII: THE BEGINNING

In the event, the Type IA U-boat emerged as two craft rather than four, designated *U 25* and *U 26*, owing to a preference for an evolving design—MVB VII. Further, in the light of the recent Anglo-German Naval Treaty (or, at least, the clauses concerning submarines that Germany had in mind to insist upon), a radical revision of the U-boat building programme could be contemplated. The programme of 1935 therefore envisaged a fleet comprising 24 of the small coastal submarines and twelve of the larger ocean-going type.

Building proceeded, stockpiles of materials and components having been made and yards readied some time before in anticipation of the rebirth; indeed, hardly was the ink dry on the Anglo-German Naval Agreement than the Weddigen Flotilla, comprising a handful of Type II coastal U-boats (and named after the World War I commander of *U 9*, which sank the British cruisers *Hogue*, *Aboukir* and *Cressy* in the space of little more than an hour one September evening in 1914), was formed.

Ambitious as it was, the submarine-building programme paled in comparison with the grandiose ideas (Plan 'Z') espoused by the German High Command for a big-gun, blue-water navy with a standing reminiscent of the Hochsee-flotte of World War I. The result was that

Type VII U-Boats: Outline specifications

	Type VII	Type VIIB	Type VIIC	Type VIID	Type VIIF
Displacement (surfaced, tons)	626	753	761	965	1,084
Displacement (submerged, tons)	745	857	865	1,080	1,181
Length (oa, ft-in)	211-7	218-2	220-2	252-4	254-7
Beam (max, ft-in)	19-0	20-4	20-4	21-0	23-11
Draught (max, ft-in)	14-5	15-5	15-9	16-5	16-0
Machinery (diesel, = output)	2 = 2,320hp	2 = 2,800hp	2 = 2,800hp	2 = 2,800hp	2 = 2,800hp
Machinery (electric, = output	2 = 750kW	2 == 750kW	2 = 750kW	2 = 750kW	2 = 750kW
Top speed (surfaced, knots)	16	17.2	17	16	17
Top speed (submerged, knots)	8	8	7.6	7.3	8
Range (surfaced, miles@knots)	4,300@12	6,500@12	6,500@12	8,100@12	9,500@12
Range (submerged, miles@knots)	90@4	90@4	80@4	69@4	75@4
Armament (torpedo tubes, bow/stern)*	4/1	4/1	4/1	4/1	4/1
No of torpedoes × calibre (cm)*	11 × 53.3	14 × 53.3	14 × 53.3	14 × 53.3	41 × 53.3
Gun armament†	1 × 8.8cm + 1 × 2cm	1 × 8.8cm + 1 × 2cm	1 × 8.8cm + 1 × 2cm	1 × 8.8cm + 1 × 2cm	1 × 8.8cm + 1 × 2cm
Mine stowage‡	22 × TMA or 33 TMB	26 × TMA or 39 × TMB	26 × TMA or 39 × TMB	26 × TMA or 39 × TMB + 15 × SMA	–
Complement (officers + men)*	4 + 40–56	4 + 40–56	4 +40–56	4 + 40	4 + 42

* There were some variations from these standard figures.
† There were great variations in the surface armament, particularly towards the latter stages of the war—see 'Appearance' section.
‡ Mines could be carried only in lieu of torpedoes except in the Type VIID, whose SMAs were carried in special mine chutes amidships.

COURTESY DAG PUBLICATIONS

Karl Dönitz, appointed, first, commander of the Weddigen Flotilla and then C-in-C U-Boats, struggled to get acceptance of his ideas for an expansion of his fleet. Such was his determination, however, that, eventually, his will to a large extent prevailed, driven by the growing reality after the outbreak of war that here was a weapon that at the same time could be produced in large numbers—and swiftly—and was extremely cost-effective in terms of its impact on the enemy's merchant shipping (and hence his ability to wage war); it would be, in short, the most important element in the Kriegsmarine's arsenal.

The first batch of Type VII U-boats—*U 27* to *U 36*, consecutively—began to be commissioned in 1936 (their characteristics are summarised in the accompanying table). The design, by Dr Friedrich Schürer, showed a single cylindrical pressure hull of carbon steel with separate bow and stern sections welded into position, within a stream-lined outer casing topped by an upper deck and conning tower. The main diving tank was located amidships, with additional trim tanks forward and aft. External saddle tanks disposed symmetrically to port and starboard and functioning for fuel/ballast release gave the Type VII its characteristic bulged appearance. Along the length of the hull, forward and aft, were rows of free-flooding drainage slots. The pressure hull comprised essentially six compartments—from stern to stem, the motor room; the main engine room; the warrant officers' quarters; the control room; the officers' quarters; and the forward torpedo room and crew accommodation. The torpedo armament consisted of eleven 53.3cm torpedoes or 22 mines, launched via four reloadable tubes forward; there was also a stern tube, situated externally, non-reloadable and usable only when the boat was on the surface. The gun armament comprised a single 8.8cm deck gun forward of the

Above: *U 29*, a Type VII (i.e., VIIA) in a heavy sea, early summer 1940. It was this boat that sank the British aircraft carrier *Courageous* in the opening weeks of the war. The highly visible conning tower numerals were deleted prior to the opening of hostilities,

COURTESY LAWRENCE PATERSON

Left: *U 30*, depicted in a poor-quality photograph which nevertheless show clearly the distinctive above-water stern torpedo tube of the first Type VII boats, and also the sharp flare of the conning tower structure brought about by the after bridge platform.

conning tower and a single (C 30) 2cm Flak aft of it, both weapons being mounted on the casing deck.

THE TYPE VIIB

The shortcomings of the first Type VII, which were either known at the outset or quickly became apparent after the boats started to enter service in 1938, were largely addressed in a revised design, the Type VIIB. The stern was reworked and lengthened by some 2m and twin rudders replaced the single, improving the boat's turning radius and permitting the after torpedo tube to be relocated (and reloaded) underwater. A considerable increase in range was brought about by massively expanding the capacity of the saddle tanks (by some 500 per cent, to 42½ tons), whilst a small increase in speed was achieved by fitting superchargers to the diesel engines. The extended stern also permitted some small additional fuel capacity and the installation of S-Gerät (*Such Gerät*, i.e. 'Search Apparatus') listening equipment. Despite these modifications, the boats' standard displacement rose only marginally.

WORKHORSE OF THE ATLANTIC

The Type VIIBs, of which two dozen were built, were very successful in service during the early part of the Second World War, but their importance was to be overshadowed by their successor, the Type VIIC, which was eventually to become the submarine produced in greater numbers than any other, before or since.

Not only was there original improvement over the Type VIIB, but as the war developed this version of the design would be upgraded and modified into a number of sub-types in an attempt to deal with the evolving threat from Allied warships and aircraft.

The fuel tanks amidships were enlarged yet again, raising capacity by about 5 tons, and a minuscule (0.6m) increase in overall length was necessary to allow for a larger control room and conning tower. A small purification plant for the engine oil was added, to enhance reliability, and small negative-buoyancy tanks, one either side, were introduced to improve diving times. There were also some adjustments to the controls and to the electrical systems.

Construction of the Type VIIC began in 1938 and the first boat was commissioned in 1940. Building continued throughout the war, despite (or perhaps because of) the arrival on to the scene of new, advanced-technology submarines. The grand total of Type VII U-boats built was about 650 (sources vary as to the precise figure, generally because of the effect of Allied air raids on 'completed' boats and what exactly constituted the latter).

UPGRADES

Although the essential geometry and layout of the Type VII remained unchanged during the war, improved equipment and various additions were introduced as the years wore on and losses in U-boats rose. These addressed

Below: *U 48* takes on stores. This particular Type VIIB became a celebrated boat, commanded for some time by Herbert Schultze and by the end of the war (when she was scuttled) responsible for sinking over 300,000 tons of Allied shipping. In this photograph it is evident that a prolonged patrol has taken its toll on the paintwork, notably on the conning tower, which also features a mass of crew-inspired artwork and slogans.

COURTESY LAWRENCE PATERSON

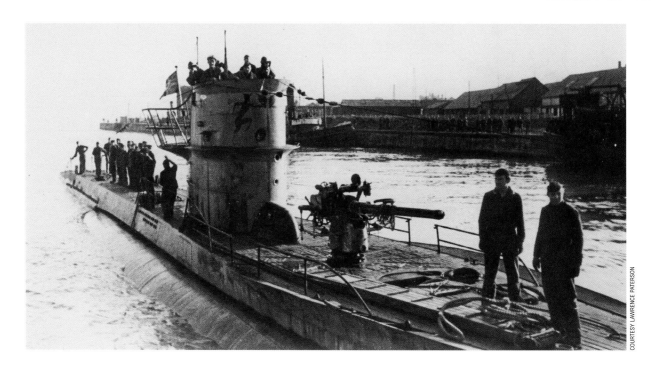

both the underwater threat and that from the air.

To meet advances in underwater detection and increasingly potent anti-submarine weapons, there was one obvious solution—improve the diving capability of the U-boat, especially the depths to which it could proceed. The basic Type VII could dive to 150m with hull failure predicted at 250m (although in practice this was often exceeded). The naval mathematicians therefore got to work and recommended various weight-saving measures to enable the pressure hull to be formed from 21mm plate rather than the existing 18.5mm gauge; in this way, no major upheaval would be introduced into the production pro-

Above: *U 552* was a standard Type VIIC. As the war progressed and surface attacks by U-boats became increasingly infrequent, the deck-mounted 8.8cm gun was unshipped from most of the fleet.

Above: An exchange of information via megaphone between two Type VIIC U-boat commanders—a basic but nevertheless secure means of communication.

Left: *U 372* (far left) from forward and *U 564* from aft. The latter was one of the many U-boats to fall victim to air attack in the Bay of Biscay.

cess then in place and, as importantly, no deterioration in performance would result from increased weight. The stronger steel could withstand much greater stresses and allowed a depth of 180m to be reached safely (failure now being predicted at 300m). This depth was certainly beyond the reach of Allied depth charges and was considered likely to remain so for the near future; moreover, the extra 30m offered extra time and opportunity for the boat to evade the slowly descending charges launched at it by the enemy. Additional benefits were the fact that asdic detection becomes more difficult as the target goes deeper; and the new hull's greater resistance to damage.

The modified boat was known as the VIIC/41 and amongst other minor changes featured a redesigned (rather wider) forepeak and a 13cm extension to the bow for improved seakeeping and entry. The first of these upgraded Type VIIs joined the fleet in summer 1943.

THE THREAT FROM THE AIR

It has often been remarked that the Type VII U-boat, for all its capabilities—and the vast Allied tonnages sunk notwithstanding—was not so much a submarine as a submersible: that is, it could not voyage for extended periods beneath the sea, having to spend by far the majority of the time on the surface in order to take in the air necessary to recharge

---

Type VII U-Boats: Hull Numbers

Type VII	*U 27–U 36* (10 boats)
Type VIIB	*U 45–U 55, U 73–U 76, U 83–U 87, U 99–U 102* (24 boats)
Type VIIC	*U 69–U 72, U 77–U 82, U 88–U 98, U 132–U 136, U 201–U 212, U 221–U 232, U 235–U 291, U 301–U 316, U 331–U 394, U 396–U 458, U 465–U 473, U 475–U 486, U 551–U 607, U 609–U 615, U 617–U 683, U 701–U 722, U 731–U 768, U 771–U 779, U 821–U 822, U 825–U 828, U 901–U 905, U 907, U 921–U 930, U 951–U 994, U 1007–U 1010, U 1013–U 1025, U 1051–U 1058, U 1063–U 1065, U 1101–U 1106, U 1131–U 1132, U 1161–U 1162, U 1172, U 1191–U 1210* (605 boats)
Type VIIC/41	*U 292–U 300, U 317–U 330, U 687–U 698, U 723–U 730, U 909–U 912, U 829–U 840, U 931–U 936, U 995–U 1006, U 1107–U 1110, U 1163–U 1170, U 1271–U 1279, U 1301–U 1308* (106 boats)
Type VIIC/42	None built
Type VIID	*U 213–U 218* (6 boats)
Type VIIE	None built
Type VIIF	*U 1059–U 1062* (4 boats)

Note: Sources give differing figures for the Type VIIC and Type VIIC/41; many of the boats (especially those of later construction) were completed but never commissioned, frequently as a result of Allied bombing raids on they yards at which they were built.

its batteries and keep its main diesel engines running. The problem was that in transiting from homeport to attack position the U-boat, if only to make reasonable way and reasonable distance, had to proceed surfaced, thereby laying itself open to air attack; with the advent of radar, this became an extremely hazardous undertaking.

Two lines of development were followed in an attempt to overcome this difficulty—equipping the boats with more and more anti-aircraft guns (to the ultimate extent that a number of Type VIICs were converted into 'Flak boats', whose sole purpose was to combat aerial attack); and the *Schnorchel*.

First proposed by a Dutch naval officer, Lieutenant-Commander Wichers (though being investigated at the same time by Helmut Walter), the *Schnorchel* was a hollow, extendible mast capable of drawing air into the interior of the U-boat whilst the latter was submerged, a system of valves and flaps in the head ensuring that water ingress was prevented and an adjacent tube allowing the diesel exhaust to escape. The positioning of the boat just below the surface was of course critical: two deep and no air would be ingested; too shallow and there was the danger that the conning tower would break the surface, its wash betraying the boat to enemy eyes. The margin for error was about six feet, which made the device unsuited for use in heavy seas. Ironically, of course, towards the end of the war, as *Schnorchel*-equipped U-boats began to appear in some numbers, Allied radar had been refined to the extent that a periscope (and thus a *Schnorchel*) could, given the right conditions, be detected fairly readily.

The equipping of Type VII U-boats with additional anti-aircraft weapons will be considered in a later section of this book ('Appearance'), where other 'add-ons' such as radar will also be reviewed.

CONTINUED DEVELOPMENT

The one other major development of the Type VII (although there were several dead-ends, as discussed below) was the Type VIID. This was a dedicated mine-laying submarine, capable of discharging the large SMA mine via chutes as well as ejecting TMA or TMB torpedo-diameter mines from the torpedo tubes in the standard fashion for the Type VII family. The modification was facilitated by the straightforward expedient of inserting an addition 9.8m long hull section immediately abaft the control room equipped with five downward-slanting shafts open to the sea below and inaccessible from within the U-boat, each chute being loaded with three mines prior to the U-boat's departure for a patrol. The remaining space created by the extra compartment was utilised to the full, accommodating compensating tanks and additional diesel-oil bunkerage. Six U-boats of this model were built, and they could operate as standard Type VIICs in terms of capability, although their performance was degraded somewhat as a result of the modification.

In an effort to extend the range and patrol times of the ocean-going U-boat fleet a small number of Type VIIs were completed as F-model supply boats, designed to rendezvous with attack boats whilst the latter were on patrol and resupply them with torpedoes—a capability that in the standard Type XIV *Milchkuh* replenishment boat was severely limited. As in the Type VIID, an extra hull section was introduced abaft conning tower, 10.5m long and, incidentally and usefully, permitting more capacious saddle tanks. There was space enough for twenty-four torpedoes and some extra crew accommodation, and, as with the Type VIID, the boats

Left: A photograph believed to depict the Type VIIC/41 *U 977*, surrendered after the war at La Plata. The C/41 sub-type could dive to greater depths than the VIIC thanks to its strengthened pressure hull; externally, it differed principally in terms of minor changes to the contours of the bow.

COURTESY DAG PUBLICATIONS

COURTESY DAG PUBLICATIONS

Right: *U 977* was on patrol at the time of the German surrender in May 1942 but her commander, Heinz Schäffer, decided to make for Argentina, where she was surrendered after a voyage lasting 108 days and including a 66-day-long underwater stint using the *Schnorchel* (which, reportedly, strained the sanity of many of the crew members). The boat was later transferred to US custody.

Right: *U 1171*, a late-production Type VIIC/41, probably here at Stavanger following her surrender to the Allies at the end of the war. The *Schnorchel* is prominent in this photograph: when not in use it retracted forwards into a housing within the main deck.

had a full combat capability; indeed, it was considerably enhanced, for the extra torpedoes could of course be used by the boat herself.

NOT PROCEEDED WITH

The C variant (including the C/41) accounted for some 95 per cent of all Type VII production, the remaining 5 per cent being made up of VIIs, VIIBs, VIIDs and VIIFs. However, a number of other variants were investigated although none of these reached fleet service.

Following the C/41, it was proposed that this concept be developed with a view to taking U-boats to even greater depths—to over 200m as a matter of procedure and to more than double that before hull failure would ensue. However, the equipment at the metal mills was working to the limits of its tolerance and nothing heavier than 28mm could be manufactured in steel plate. The alternative was to use armour plate, but the significant weight increase that

this material involved could not be accommodated within the basic Type VII design and, even though contracts began to be issued (in February 1943; nearly 200 of these C/42 boats were eventually ordered), the project was abandoned owing to ever-changing demands for modifications to the design (boosted engines, greater dimensions) and the gradual realisation that the parameters for the latter could be satisfactorily met by the new Type XXI. It is recorded that the Soviets completed a number of unfinished Type VIIC/42s after the war, though to what configuration is unknown. A version of the C/42 equipped with half a dozen bow torpedo tubes and two at the stern was designated C/43 but was theoretical only.

The other 'paper' project was the Type VIIE, which was designed to test lightweight Deutz V12 two-stroke diesel engines. Difficulties with the new powerplants, however, led to its cancellation.

COURTESY LAWRENCE PATERSON

Careers

THE deployment of U-boats during the Second World War posed what was arguably the most vexing single problem facing British (and, to a lesser extent American) naval strategists and technicians; unlike the threat from German surface ships—ranging from the big capital ships, through the 'pocket battleships' (see *ShipCraft 1*) and the armed surface raiders to the small coastal vessels, including S-boats—that from beneath the waters of the Atlantic involved large numbers of vessels, with steadily increasing capabilities and employing evolving tactics, and demanding specialist countermeasures which sheer numbers of anti-submarine vessels alone could not counter.

In late 1939, at the beginning of the conflict, there was the inevitability of a re-run of the chaos caused by sub-marines in the First World War, though at this stage the German U-boat fleet was relatively small and, it was considered, 'containable'. As the months progressed and the Atlantic War unfolded, however, the expansion of the fleet caused more and more serious difficulty until a point was reached, round about October 1940, when the destruction of British and Allied merchant shipping by U-boats reached such appalling levels that it threatened Great Britain's continuing ability to promote *any* form of effective warfare.

From about late 1941, slowly and inexorably, and despite the continuing increase in U-boat numbers, the British and their allies started to gain the upper hand in the Atlantic War. The reasons were manifold, each very significant in itself but each no more than a

Right: Type VIICs at Narvik following the successful German attacks on the Russian convoy PQ.17, July 1942.

Below: *U 47* at Wilhelms-haven on 17 October 1939, three days after pulling off one of the great *coups* of the war—the sinking of the battleship HMS *Royal Oak* in Scapa Flow, the Royal Navy's fleet anchorage in the Orkney Islands.

COURTESY DAG PUBLICATIONS

COURTESY DAG PUBLICATIONS

Below: *U 556*, a Type VIIC, at Lorient on 30 May 1941. This U-boat would be lost off Greenland four weeks later in operations against convoy HX.133: having been depth-charged by Allied corvettes, she was surrounded and sunk by gunfire. Her commander at the time, *Kapitänleutnant* Wohlfarth, is depicted on page 2 of this book.

component part of the changing balance of power.

TACTICS AND STRATEGY

The groundwork for the deployment of the Type VII was laid prior to the outbreak of war when the ten Type VIIs were combined to form the Saltzwedel Flotilla. Experience with these boats showed that they lacked range but otherwise represented a satisfactory compromise amongst the various conflicting requirements, which included stability and seakeeping, potency, habitability, speed and diving capabilities.

Their impact on the conflict was immediate: on 3 September—the very day that Britain and Germany commenced hostilities—*U 30* sank the passenger liner *Athenia* (in error, according to the German U-Boat Command), whilst shortly afterwards the Royal Navy

COURTESY DAG PUBLICATIONS

Another view of *U 556* at Lorient, 30 May 1941. About half the crew are visible topside as the boat approaches her berth; one man is emerging from one of the torpedo store access hatches.

COURTESY DAG PUBLICATIONS

fleet aircraft carrier *Courageous* was sunk by sister-boat *U 29*.

These successes and other early victories, dramatic as they were, came about as each side probed for weaknesses in the enemy's defences. They were the result of 'lone wolf' attacks—perforce, since Dönitz, despite his hard lobbying of the German Naval High Command, had only a few dozen boats at his disposal during the opening months of the war, of which perhaps half were available for operations at any one moment.

In terms of tactics, the received wisdom prior to the outbreak of war was for the attacker, if the target was armed, to stand off, submerged, some 2,500–3,000 yards in order to fire torpedoes: closing the enemy to reduce the range was a desirable option if the target was a merchantman. The caution was brought about by the existence of asdic, and the consequent risk of detection; the great drawback of long-range firing was of course that the margin of error was huge, and even if a spread of torpedoes were launched the chances of missing the victim were high. Very quickly following the deployment of the U-boats, however, commanders began to test Dönitz's theory that the risk of detection by asdic was seriously overrated, and it was discovered that close-quarter firing (from ranges as little as 500 yards) could be carried out with a fair measure of impunity.

Surface attack became a more common tactic as the war unfolded. The U-boat's top speed of some 15 knots was significantly higher than that of the typical convoy (whose speed was determined by that of the slowest ship) and, indeed, than that of many escort vessels, and so the odds on evading retribution were high—especially at night. Moreover, surface attack, with gunfire, kept valuable torpedoes available for those opportunities where underwater attack was the only option.

With increasing numbers of U-boats joining the flotillas from early 1940 onwards, the tactic of the 'wolf pack', a 'live' concept even as far back as the First World War, could be put into effect. The advantages to commanders of having several boats loose amongst a convoy instead of merely their own are plain; and, as well as overwhelming the hapless merchantmen with numbers, the opportunity for confusion, if attacks could be launched simultaneously and from several directions, was fertile indeed. All depended upon the convoy being sighted—and with greater numbers of U-boats spread loosely across its projected course the chances of its being detected were very good—then the boats in the pack could be summoned and concentrated.

U-BOAT MEN

From an early core of First World War veterans supplemented by recruits from the UAS (Ubootsabwehrschule) set up in the autumn of 1933, the U-boat arm was increasingly manned by young men, almost all of them volunteers, instilled with the spirit of the times, highly motivated and trained to a high standard of

Right: A Type VII makes headway across choppy seas. This is a postwar photograph, and the boat is under Allied authority.

proficiency. Such was the lure of the Service, and the prestige in which the crews basked, that there was never a shortage of crews; even during the latter years of the war, when the fortunes of the U-boat arm were plummeting and the crews' survival rates were distinctly depressing, men continued to come forward.

In recognition, perhaps, of the unique dangers of their work, and certainly of the high levels of competence that were required to carry out their duties, U-boat men were paid well and looked after whilst in port. Whilst on board their boats, crews quickly discovered a respectful informality towards superior officers that would not have been tolerated in other branches of the Kriegsmarine, and a special camaraderie not evident aboard surface ships. It could only be thus: with upwards of 50 men, possibly, all jostling for space in a cylinder 150 feet long by not much more than head height. Space was limited, comfort at a premium and luxury nonexistent.

THE COMMANDERS

It was inevitable, given the scale of the war, the period over which hostilities stretched, the size of the U-boats' hunting grounds and the defencelessness (or unpreparedness) of most of the targets, that tallies of victims would be made and 'aces' declared. Several U-boat commanders totted up huge tonnages of merchantmen, frequently on account of their skill as leaders and tacticians but

sometimes, it has to be said, as a result of good fortune in being in the right place at the right time, especially if they were a member of a 'wolf pack' and were lucky enough to survive enemy action and continue their operations. Men like *Fregattenkapitäne* Erich Topp (35 vessels totalling 192,600 tons) and Heinrich Lehmann-Willenbrock (25; 183,000) and *Kapitänleutnante* Otto Kretschmer (56; 300,000), Günther Prien (31; 192,000) and Joachim Schepke (37; 145,000) were all outstanding commanders, and were richly decorated for their achievements.

Held in even greater esteem by the Germans were those few commanders who, by dint of careful planning and

CARSTEN HEINTZE

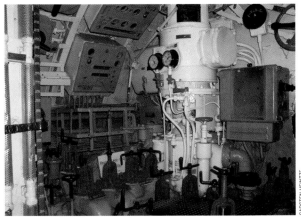

CARSTEN HEINTZE

CARSTEN HEINTZE

CARSTEN HEINTZE

CARSTEN HEINTZE

GERHARD KOOP

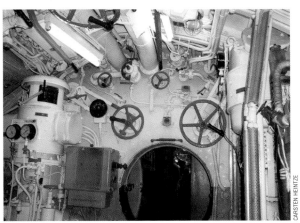

CARSTEN HEINTZE

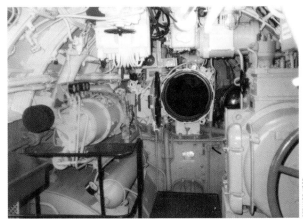

GERHARD KOOP

Left: The preserved Type VIIC at Laboe (see pages 62–63) offers visitors the opportunity to sample the interior of a U-boat. While the noise, smell, heat, grime, exhilaration and fear of a U-boat patrol cannot be reproduced, the exhibit does convey the cramped nature of the accommodation, which of course crews had to endure for weeks on end. Above and right: The danger of air attack, particularly when within range of Allied air bases, was an ever-present headache for U-boat commanders. These boats are both Type VIICs, that below being *U 134*, seen here on 8 July 1943.

particular daring, accomplished the spectacular. Prien, it has been argued, was the greatest U-boat captain of all time: not only was his tonnage of merchantmen outstandingly high, but before he set about making his contribution to the toll of sunken vessels in the Atlantic he had pulled off the *coup* of the war when, on 14 October 1939, his boat, U 47, entered the Royal Navy's anchorage at Scapa Flow in the Orkney Islands having evaded all the defences and sank the battleship *Royal Oak*.

More fortuitously, the names Schuhart, Guggenberger, Rosenbaum and Tiesenhausen have entered the annals of naval history for these men's achievements in sinking major British warships—the aircraft carriers *Courageous*, *Ark Royal* and *Eagle* and the battleship *Barham*, respectively.

One more Type VII commander may be highlighted—Albrecht Brandi, who seemed to specialise in hazardous approaches to warships. His achievements were apparent principally in the Mediterranean, where he accounted for two destroyers and a minelayer, damaged a number of other warships and mounted several other, unsuccessful attacks.

DEMISE

From small-scale but sometimes spectacular beginnings, the war waged by the German U-Boat Service steadily grew in intensity and effectiveness as the numbers of boats available to Dönitz increased, strategy and tactics were re-

fined and torpedoes were improved, in terms of both reliability and potency (particularly the widespread introduction of the G7e, slower than the earlier G7a but wakeless). However, although by the second year of the war the boats were promising to win a lasting victory over the North Atlantic merchant traffic, the Allies in due time began to gain

the upper hand, to the extent that by the summer of 1943 the U-Boat Service was a defeated force, the brand-new-technology Type XXIs that were just coming into service notwithstanding.

The reasons were manifold—the growing material strength of the Allies (in particular, the industrial muscle of the United States, which made available anti-submarine ships and aircraft in unprecedented numbers, and the closing of the 'air gap' by means of very long-range patrol aircraft); the Allies' rapid strides in new technology, including advances in HF/DF, radar and asdic (sonar); and their new, more potent weaponry, including depth charges that could sink faster and detonate at greater depths and mortars that could be projected ahead of the attacking ship

('Hedgehog') instead of fired over the stern. Underpinning all of these strides, however, was the fortuitous (and secret) capture, in May 1941, of a German Enigma machine from *U 110* (a Type IXB) off Greenland, which enabled the British to read the 'Hydra' codes in which messages to the U-Boat Service were transmitted: despite the ten-month 'black-out' in code-breaking that followed the Germans' changing their code to 'Triton' in February 1942, this event, and the expertise in the intelligence war that rapidly developed as a result, was the single most important factor in the eventual Allied victory, enabling, to the complete bafflement of the Germans, convoys to be routed and countermeasures to be positioned to the maximum effect.

Above: Desperate problems called for desperate measures, and a number of Type VIICs were fitted out exclusively for the anti-aircraft role. This is *U 441*.

Below: The Type VIIC *U 570* was captured by the British (following a surprise air attack) on 27 August 1941 and was commissioned into the Royal Navy as HMS *Graph*.

Model Products

Right: The Type VIIB and Type
VIIC U-boats from Navis-
Neptun: masterpieces in
miniature.
Below: The contents of the
Hasegawa 1/700 U-boat set,
with the Type VIIC at right and
the Type IXC in the fore-
ground.

MODELS of Type VII U-boats are readily available and range from tiny 1/1250 scale waterline miniatures to enormous 1/32 scale full-hull kits. The quality is generally high, although working models, because they need to absorb much handling, tend to lack the delicacy of their static equivalents—although, as one of the exhibits in the 'Modelmakers' Showcase' pages of this book demonstrates, it is quite possible to improve upon any radio-control model in terms of its outward appearance.

The following brief reviews, as always, are not intended to be more than very general, nor do they necessarily include all the available products.

Models

Navis-Neptun: *U 47, U 217, U 995* (1/1250)

Surely the smallest available models of U-boats, these tiny castings exhibit a tremendous amount of surface and added detail considering that each is only about 2in long. One would not go so far as to say that fittings such as periscopes and gun barrels are of scale thickness, but the fact that they are present at all is testimony to the skills of the Navis-Neptun mouldmakers.

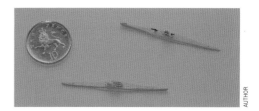

The lines of the Type VII are convincingly captured in both models and there is fine recessed detail along the hull and on the main deck; the conning towers are also very realistically moulded, with the bulwarks as thin as can be imagined bearing in mind the scale.

The Type VIIB is represented by *U 47* (what else!) and the Type VIIC by *U 995*, which lacks the 8.8cm deck gun and has two 20mms and a single 3.7cm on the 'Wintergarten'.

The models are finished in pale grey with, on *U 47*, the gun barrels picked out in black. A *very light* dry-brushing in a contrasting colour will make them even more attractive.

Sample: Courtesy Navis-Neptun

Plastic Kits

Hasegawa: Type VIIC and Type IXC U-Boats (1/700)

A pair of U-boats and a sinking freighter make up a novel and attractive little kit but one which has some faults. The main problem with the Type VII element of the kit is that the beam of the boat appears too broad for reality, and there is not very much that can be done about it without sacrificing practically all the surface detailing that the Hasegawa toomakers have provided.

17

The hull for the Type VII (and indeed that for the Type IX) is a one-piece, four-way moulding with a separate waterline flat, and the periscope assembly, guns and ensign staff are offered as separate components. However, despite the delicacy of the parts—and the mast components for the merchantman, for example, are some of the thinnest injection mouldings ever produced for a plastic kit—the two-part conning-tower assembly looks somewhat bizarre because the guard rail aft is represented by a solid, curved wall of plastic with raised exterior detailing; better by far, surely, to have omitted it altogether.

Despite the foregoing, this very simple kit is worth looking at and also has conversion potential since the Type IXC's conning tower can, with adjustment, be utilised to give variation to the Type VIIC.

Sample: Author's Collection

Heller: Type VIIC or VIIC/41 U-Boat (1/400)

To Heller's standard warship scale, this is a typically robust kit and one which has, over the years, appeared in a variety of guises. The mouldings for which the box top is illustrated here include optional parts to create an early variant of the boat with a single 20mm or a later (C/41) 'Wintergarten' version with two single 20mms and a single 3.7cm and *sans* 8.8cm; other releases based on these tools may differ. The hull mould-

Type VII U-Boats: Kits and models

	Manufacturer	Scale	Hull	Remarks
Type VIIB (*U 47*)	Navis-Neptun	1/1250	Waterline	Metal model, ready assembled
Type VIIC (*U 995*)	Navis-Neptun	1/1250	Waterline	Metal model, ready assembled
Type VIID (*U 217*)	Navis-Neptun	1/1250	Waterline	Metal model, ready assembled
Type VIIC	Hasegawa	1/700	Waterline	Plastic kit, boxed with Type IXC and 'sinking' merchant ship
Type VIIC	Heller	1/400	Full hull	Plastic kit
Type VIIC (*U 576/995*)	Heller	1/400	Full hull	Plastic kit
Type VIIC/41 (*U 576*)	Heller	1/400	Full hull	Plastic kit
Type VIIB (*U 84*)	Mirage Hobby	1/400	Full hull	Plastic kit
Type VIIC	Mirage Hobby	1/400	Full hull	Plastic kit
Type VIIC (*U 570*)	Mirage Hobby	1/400	Full hull	Plastic kit; Turm I configuration
Type VIIC (*U 571*)	Mirage Hobby	1/400	Full hull	Plastic kit; basic configuration with 8.8cm gun
Type VIIC (*U 673*)	Mirage Hobby	1/400	Full hull	Plastic kit; Turm II configuration
Type VIIC (*U 826*)	Mirage Hobby	1/400	Full hull	Plastic kit; Turm IV configuration, *Schnorchel*
Type VIIC (*U 1064*)	Mirage Hobby	1/400	Full hull	Plastic kit; includes *Schnorchel*
Type VIIC/41 (*U 295*)	Mirage Hobby	1/400	Full hull	Plastic kit; includes two *Biber*s
Type VIIC	Artitec	1/350	Full hull	Resin kit
Type VII (*U 35*)	Blue Water Navy	1/350	Full hull	Resin kit
Type VIIC	Blue Water Navy	1/350	Full hull	Resin kit
Type VIIC	Combat Subs	1/350	Full hull	Resin kit
Type VIIC	Seawolf	1/350	Full hull	Resin kit
Type VIIC	Tom's Modelworks	1/350	Full hull	Resin kit
Type VIIC (*U 581*)	Academy	1/150	Full hull	Plastic kit with motor option and 'diving' capability
Type VIIC	Doyusha	1/150	Full hull	Working model (motorised)
Type VIIB (*U 47*)	Revell	1/125	Full hull	Plastic kit, 'cut away' to show interior features
Type VIIB (*U 99*)	Revell	1/125	Full hull	Plastic kit
Type VIIB (*U 47*)	Amati	1/72	Full hull	Resin kit
Type VIIC	Combat Models	1/72	Full hull	Vacform kit
Type VIIC	Revell	1/72	Full hull	Plastic kit
Type VIIB	Krick	1/60	Full hull	ABS kit for radio control
Type VIIB (*U 47*)	Robbe	1/40	Full hull	Fibreglass kit for radio control
Type VIIC	Accurate Armour	1/35	Waterline	Resin kit
Type VIIC	Andrea Miniatures	1/32	Full hull	Resin/metal/photo-etch kit
Type VIIC (*U 556*)	Andrea Miniatures	1/32	–	Resin kit of conning tower only
Type VIIB (*U 47*)	32nd Parallel	1/32	Full hull	Fibreglass kit, for radio-controlled model
Type VIIC	OTW	1/32	Full hull	Fibreglass and etched-metal kit, for radio controlled model

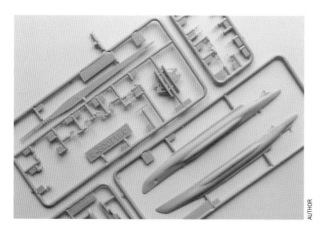

AUTHOR

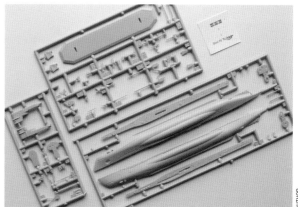

AUTHOR

Above: Spreads of parts for the Heller Type VIIC (left) and Mirage Hobby *U 826* (right) kits.
Right: Mirage Hobby Type VIIC, modelled by Larry Goodell.
Below: Five more box tops from the Mirage Hobby range of Type VII U-boat plastic kits.

LARRY GOODELL

ing is full, split longitudinally as one may expect, with a separate main deck and each conning tower in two halves.

It is interesting to compare this kit with that offered by Hasegawa, and it must be observed that the finesse of the latter is considerably greater and the detailing sharper—even though the Japanese kit is about half the size of the French. One upshot of this is that Heller's 3.7cm and 8.8cm gun interpretations are within microns of being exactly the same size.

In general dimensions and appearance the kit is satisfactory, and if 1/400 enthusiasts can get to grips with some superdetailing the end result will be a very attractive little model. One task that will definitely have to be tackled concerns the flooding vents, which are shown as raised tabs, and rather unevenly at that.

Sample: Author's Collection

Mirage Hobby: Type VIIC U-Boats (various) (1/400 scale)

One of the most fundamental technical changes to be made to injection-moulded kits over the last twenty-five years or so has been the wholesale switch from raised detail to recessed detail. (the main reason being that the market has changed—'grown up'—and become both more demanding and, relatively speaking, more wealthy).

This series of kits, six in all representing Type VIIs, from a relatively new company in Poland, has been well received in the modelling press, and it is easy to see why: very well detailed and with a crisp, clean fit, the parts are engineered in up-to-date fashion with neatly recessed panel lines and flooding holes. As with the Heller kit, there is no encouragement from the manufacturer to produce a waterline model from the parts, but of course this can be accomplished without undue difficulty by carefully sawing through the hull halves prior to assembly and provid-

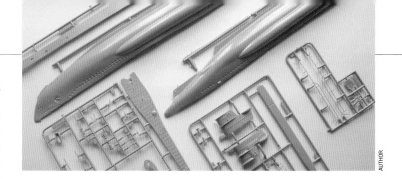

AUTHOR

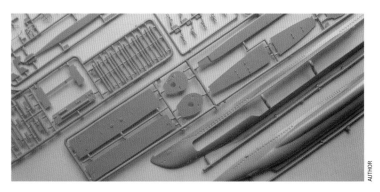

AUTHOR

ing some added rigidity by means of a plastic-card 'base'.

The various Type VIICs available from Mirage are briefly summarised in the table on page 18; this particular kit produces a Turm IV configuration with *Schnorchel*, FuMO 30 radar antenna and two unshielded single 20mms and a shielded 3.7cm on an extended 'Wintergarten'.

The instruction sheets for these kit are not, perhaps, as clear as they could be: the location points for the various fittings will be a touch mysterious to the uninitiated, whilst the pale grey pointers for the painting guide are so pale as to have virtually disappeared.

Samples: Courtesy Mirage Hobby

Revell: *U 99* (1/125)

This is now a quite elderly product, and compared with Revell's current offering in a much larger scale (see below) it will nowadays be a disappointment. The detailing on the hull is sparse, the fit less than perfect and the presence of 'flash' on the parts betrays the kit's quarter-century-old origins.

These points aside, this representation of Kretschmer's boat does build into a quite convincing model, and some aspects—for example the deck slots and the 8.8cm gun— are pleasing. Care will have to be taken when cleaning up the rail components, to avoid breakage, and indeed affixing them.

A small decal sheet provides an ensign and some victory pennants, plus bow plate identification numbers.

Sample: Author's Collection

Revell: *U 47* (1/125)

A later kit than the foregoing, this one has most of its basic parts in common with its predecessor but the port half of the hull and the (entirely redesigned) conning tower have large sections removed so as to cnable some of the interior fittings to be displayed. Whilst the

latter are not by any stretch of the imagination 'superdetailed', their installation gives a good basic appreciation of the inboard profile of a Type VIIB (and, for that matter, a Type VIIC of course). Curiously, although the *U 47* kit contains well over 50 per cent more plastic than that of the U 99 and has well over twice as many parts, both seem to retail for about the same price.

Amongst the additional parts are bulkheads, engines, reload torpedoes (forward and aft), bunks, mouldings displaying control consoles and, not least, some 1/125 scale figures, one of which depicts Prien himself at the periscope. The various dials etc are picked out on the model by means of decals.

Both these 1/125 scale Revell kits are depicted as built-up models in the 'Showcase' section of this book.

Sample: Author's Collection

Above: Revell offer two U-boats in 1/125 scale, *U 99* (top) and *U 47*, the latter with 'cutaway' features and interior parts.

Below: Revell also market a Type VIIC U-boat: released in 2004, this has been widely—and deservedly—acclaimed in the modelling press.

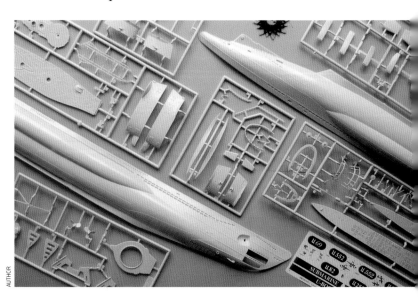

AUTHOR

Right: Early stages in the construction of Revell's big U-boat, by Peter Hall. Note the paper template for the port upper torpedo-tube door in place—the prototype stage in the production of the WEM brass-etched fret.

Below: The Revell U-boat completed, by Michael Leuchtenberger. For further views of Michael's model see pages 30–31.

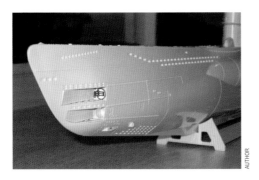

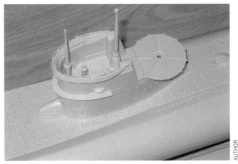

Revell: Type VIIC U-Boat (1/72)

Judging by its reception, this kit must be one of the most popular of recent times; it was certainly eagerly anticipated. It is also a very fine product, and representative of Revell at their best, giving the plastic kit builder exactly what he or she requires—general overall accuracy, a straightforward assembly procedure without any gimmicks and, for what is on offer, a reasonable price tag. This sensible approach means that a very acceptable model results merely from building and finishing the kit in a careful manner; but it also gives enormous scope to those who wish to lavish time and skill (and, perhaps, further outlay).

In essence, the kit offers two major variants in configuration—the first equipped with bow cutters and conning-tower intakes and the second without the foregoing but featuring the antenna

21

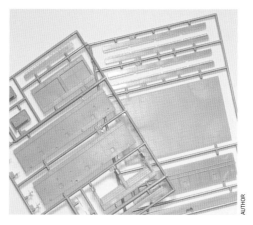

Left: Parts for Skywave's U-boat bunker kit.

fairing on the port side of the tower. Six different external finishes are provided four, involving five different boats (*U 552* appearing in either 'early' or 'late' guise).

The two-piece hull is a massive and thankfully robust moulding and the main deck is supplied in three separate parts. All flooding vents are depicted as recessed hollows, crisply delineated, and, at the very least, builders will wish to drill though those at the bow to give the correct 'see-through' effect.

The conning tower assembly is well detailed if leaving scope for many more refinements to be made as required. It comprises two 'layers', each in two halves, with a separate one-piece deck through which the periscopes are fed, the length of the latter suggesting that a reissue of the kit with 'cutaway' features might be an option for Revell in the future. The 8.8cm and 20mm AA guns are realistic, forming good bases for further detailing if required. The guard rail is delicate, and as close to scale thickness as one could wish. The decals are to an excellent standard, and cord is provided for the rig though is probably best substituted with something finer and more realistic.

Sample: Courtesy Revell GmbH

Accessory Packs

The release of Revell's 1/72 U-boat, in particular, has set off a wave of 'aftermarket' accessory sets, not only in the form of brass-etched frets for the 'superdetail' enthusiasts but also in the form of resin components and decal sheets, while for the larger-scale models a number of companies offer sets of crew figures in various poses. Meanwhile, those who specialise in the smaller scales have accessory kits to choose from too . . .

Skywave: German Navy Bunker (1/700)

Amongst a batch of diorama accessory sets emanating from Japan some 25–30 years ago was a series from the then-new company Skywave, and of particular relevance to the U-boat enthusiast was this set representing a twin bunker complex enlivened by basic interior detailing, exterior access steps, roof-mounted single and quadruple 20mms and a couple of covered four-wheel trucks.

Skywave made a big impact with the small-scale waterline modeller, and quickly gained a reputation for producing high quality kits of offbeat subjects. This one, which is extremely simple to construct, typified the company's approach.

Sample: Author's Collection

Mirage Hobby: Type VII U-Boat Photo-etched Sets (various) (1/400)

These sets have been individually designed to complement the same company's 1/400 scale plastic model kits (see above). Each measures approximately 3½in × 2in and comprises brass-

Right, upper: Photo-etched accessory sets by Mirage Hobby in 1/400 scale. Right, lower: Ulad decal sheets for the Revell 1/72 scale U-boat.

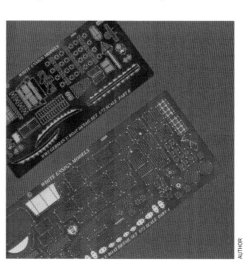

Left: Etched brass frets from the 1/72 Type VIIC U-Boat set by White Ensign Models. Right: U-boat figures from Accurate Armour in 1/35 scale—a rare foray by this renowned company into matters nautical.

Type VII U-Boats: Accessories etc.

Manufacturer	Scale	Remarks
Tom's Modelworks	1/700	Axis submarines detailing set (two German plus two Japanese)
Tom's Modelworks	1/700	Figures (120 items, various poses)
Tom's Modelworks	1/400	Detailing set for five of the six Mirage Hobby kits
Mirage Hobby	1/400	Six separate detailing sets for the same manufacturer's 1/400 scale U-boat kits
Nautilus Models	1/125	Type VIIB resin 'upgrading' kit
White Ensign Models	1/72	Brass-etched detailing set for Revell kit
Nautilus Models	1/72	Replacement deck parts in etched metal, CT platform, resin hatches etc.
Hecker & Goros	1/72	Three different white-metal sets of U-boat crew figures in various poses
Czech Master	1/72	Six different sets of resin U-boat crew figures in various poses
Houshinya	1/72	Gun barrels and periscopes in aluminium
Ulad	1/72	Various decal sheets
Accurate Armour	1/35	2cm Flak in resin, metal and etched brass
Accurate Armour	1/35	U-boat crew figures (various) in resin
Andrea Miniatures	54mm	Deck gun and crew
Andrea Miniatures	54mm	Five separate U-boat crew figures
Andrea Miniatures`	54mm	U-boat anchor
Mirage Hobby	200mm	U-boat officer in resin
Verlinden	1/4	Bust of U-boat captain

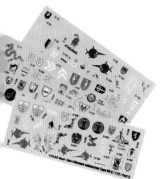

etched decking, guard rail, propellers, gun details and deck fittings.

As with the kits themselves, the instructions are somewhat vague in places, although this will matter less to experienced modellers, who may be presumed to constitute the principal market for these exquisite products.

Samples: Courtesy Mirage Hobby

White Ensign Models: Type VIIC U-Boat (1/72) (Set no PE 7203)

From a company which needs no introduction to ship and boat modelLers, this set comprises two frets offering a host of fine detail designed to complement the Revell kit. The components range from improved nct-cutters and torpedo-tube doors through hatch details and bollards to a host of items designed to add realism to the focal point of any U-boat model, the conning tower. These last include such intricacies as foot- and hand-rails for the attack periscope, vents and

grilles and radar antennas—FuMO 29, 30, 61, 'Naxos' and the Biskayakreuz—while there are also tiny brass components for detailing the 20mm gun. Not least, there are a selection of valve caps for the ballast tanks which, on account of the draw angles required for the hull mouldings in Revell's kit, could not be incorporated into the original plastic parts.

Samples: Courtesy WEM

Figures

Accurate Armour: U-Boat Crew Figures (1/35)

Accurate Armour, a small business operating from Port Glasgow in Scotland, has been producing very high quality multimedia kits and models of AFV and related subjects for almost twenty years now, both for the public and for the defence industry. It does not, therefore, specialise in naval subjects, but a number of items that are marketed—not least an extremely impressive 1/35 scale kit for a Type VII U-boat—will be of interest to the marine modeller.

These delightful resin castings comprise a U-boat commander, a deck officer and an officer in mixed dress, all bearded and with the deck officer clutching a pair of binoculars There is not a hint of flash on any of them, and a quick pass of the scalpel around the cast base and a gentle washing is all that is required before painting begins. One could not ask for better canvases than these.

Samples: Courtesy Accurate Armour

Mirage Hobby: German U-Boat Officer (200mm)

Amongst the dozen or so 200mm (1/9 scale) cast resin figures in the catalogue of this enterprising Polish company is a first-class representation of a bearded U-boat officer in exceptionally informal dress. The figure itself comprises five separate pieces, to which are added a pair of binoculars (two options are offered) and some minuscule etched-brass cap insignia. A base in the form of a section of quayside plus a bollard is also provided.

The castings have substantial plugs but minimal flash, and these and the light moulding seams will need attention before painting can be undertaken.

As with Mirage Hobby's 1/400 U-boat kits, the instructions could be improved upon: those unfamiliar with the subject will have difficulty deciding where some of the smaller parts should be located.

Sample: Courtesy Mirage Hobby

Above: The 200mm U-Boat Officer from Mirage Hobby.

RADIO-CONTROLLED MODELS

In the world of radio-control model boats, the model submariner has a hard time. Not for him the Sunday-afternoon session at the local pond lazily sending his craft back and forth across the waters, performing routine rudder movements and dodging his competitors. His boat has to sink—in a controlled manner, of course—and, furthermore, one basic error in construction can mean that the maiden voyage could be the last one!

Radio-controlled submarines are of two basic types, 'wet hull' or 'dry hull'; the former acts more like its full-size counterpart in that it has two hulls, an inner, watertight hull and an outer, free-flooding hull. With the 'dry hull' model, the outer hull is the watertight unit. Models can be further subdivided into 'dynamic' or 'static' divers, the former requiring forward motion in order that the control planes can have effect.

The 'wet hull' model is a relatively recent introduction, requiring the provision of a watertight cylinder (wtc) inside which all the running equipment can be stowed and, more importantly, kept dry. It follows that, even in these days of miniaturisation, there will be a lower limit in the size of the model that can be built. On the other hand, it is possible to exchange wtcs among different models. This form also makes for a lighter model, since strength and rigidity in the outer hull is less important than in the 'dry hull' variety inasmuch as it is not subject to differential pressures at depth and, moreover, does not require huge amounts of ballast since its displacement is that much less.

There is a wide range of kits available for working model Type VII U-boats, some basic and some highly detailed and truly authentic in appearance. As many R/C modellers will confirm, there is no reason today why working models cannot emulate their static counterparts in terms of display quality.

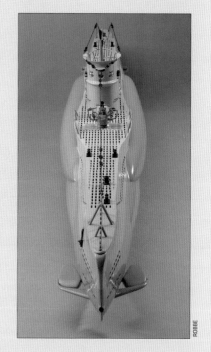

The Robbe 1/40 scale Type VIIB model; and (below) detail of the OTW 1/32 scale Type VIIC with (left) a sample from this kit's brass-etched frets.

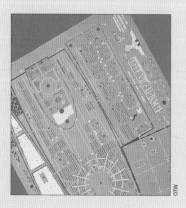

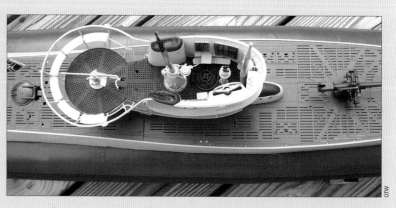

Modelmakers' Showcase

SUBMARINES of all types have immense popular appeal, and they do indeed have added attractions amongst the modelmaking fraternity. They are, generally speaking, uncomplicated in external appearance and models do not call for the addition of masses of intricate detail in order to convince; they have tended to be built in large classes, offering the modeller a wide range in terms of the choice of individual boat; they are usually well documented, which means that reliable reference material is not difficult to find; being small craft (compared with fleet warships), they can be modelled in larger scales and thereby lend themselves to the addition of well-detailed and realistic figures (and thus appeal to a separate area of modelling

GEOFF REICHELT

interest); and, lastly, they are hugely popular with the radio-control model enthusiasts, for obvious reasons.

CARSTEN HEINTZE

OTW

U 331   1/48 scale   Dan Kachur

Master modelmaker Dan Kachur, who hails from Richmond, British Columbia, specialises in building wonderful working models of submarines, many of which are on display in the Granville Island Museums complex near Vancouver. His subjects have included an intriguing model of the *Nautilus* (from the film *20,000 Leagues under the Sea*), a 72-inch working replica of the USS *Queenfish* (which made an appearance in the television series *The X-Files*), and this superb rendering of *U 331*, the U-boat that sank the battleship *Barham* in November 1941.

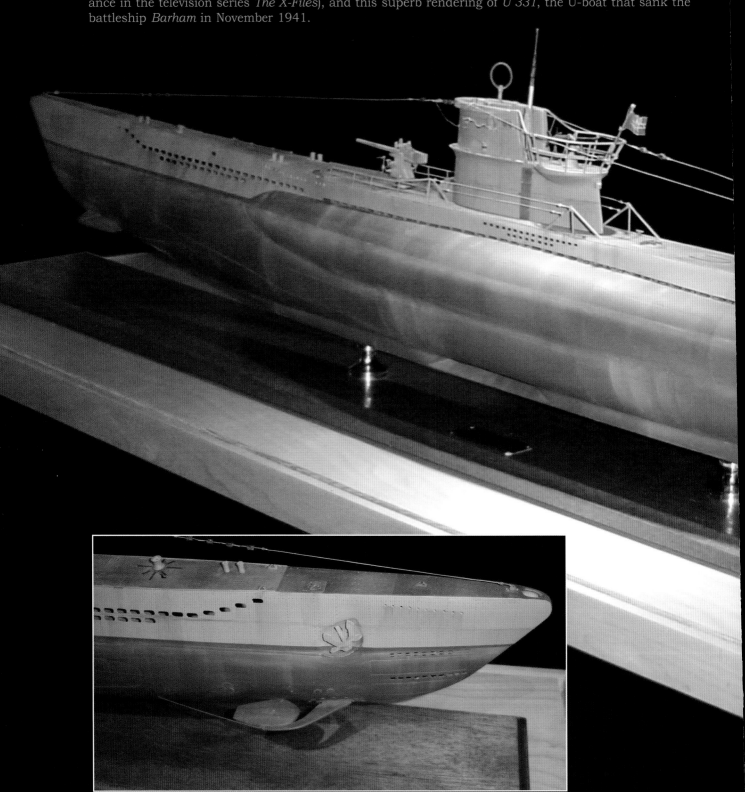

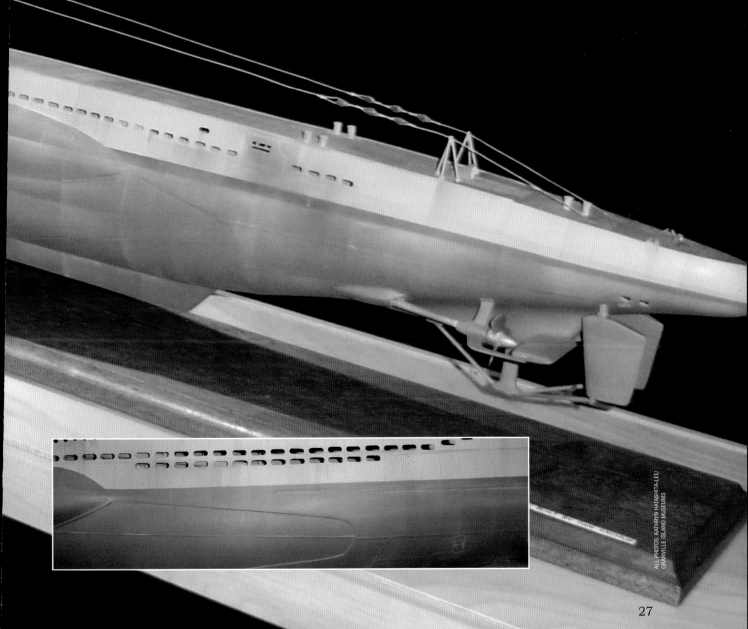

27

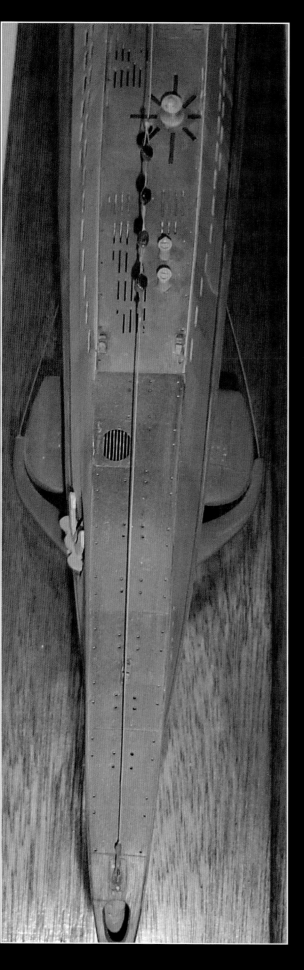

SCRATCH BUILT BY DAN KACHUR

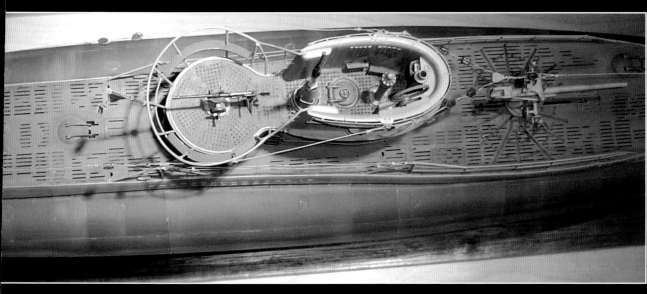

Dan's model of *U 331*, which is some 52in long, is entirely scratchbuilt. Typically, his models of submarines are produced using the traditional 'plank-on-frame' method, with a watertight fibreglass sealing system, and the fittings are hand-made from brass. Periscopes can be raised and lowered by remote (radio) control, while guns and torpedoes can be 'fired' realistically. Of course, they have a complete diving capability too, and realistic engine noise . . .

U 552   1/72 scale   Michael Leuchtenberger

Revell's big U-boat—released in early 2004 following intense speculation—is shown here as built by Michael Leuchtenberger, the well-known modelmaker from Moers, near Duisburg in Germany.

Michael is a prolific modeller, though not a man who specialises in naval subjects; in fact, this is his first attempt at a model of a U-boat. His principal interest is aircraft of the wartime and post-war eras, and he has also built some beautiful model cars and some very realistic military dioramas. His portfolio of work can be seen at Micha's Bastelstube (Micha's Hobby Room) at http://www.michas-bastelstube.de.

Michael's painting and finishing skills are to the fore here, on a model that has been built with some essential modifications (such as opened flooding holes) rather than 'straight from the box'. Of particular note also are the weathering and rusting effects, painstakingly portrayed in great detail to give a very authentic 'feel' to the model while at the same time emphasising the surface detail. The boat depicted by the model is the 'early ' version of *U 552*—a standard option in the kit—with cable cutters at the bow, minor differences concerning the conning tower, etc.

ALL PHOTOS: MICHAEL LEUCHTENBERGER

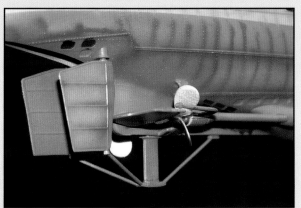

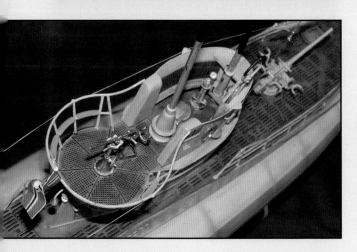

U 82 1/72 scale Dave Morrissette

Here is an excellent interpretation of the very popular Revell 1/72 scale kit, built with some corrections and added detailing (see pages 21–22 for a review of the basic kit).

Amongst the amendments Dave has worked in are the opening-up of the free-flooding holes and the addition of a simulated pressure hull, from very thin plastic card rolled into a cylinder, inside the main hull components.

Some modifications to the conning tower were made, in the interests of added realism, and the 8.8cm gun was re-fashioned to show the tompion and its attachment cable. The 2cm Flak gun was replaced using hypodermic syringe tubing and plastic card.

The model is finished in matt greys with lightly dusted black and rust coloured pastel chalk. The rigging cord supplied with the kit is rather overscale and monofilament line was substituted.

ALL PHOTOS: DAVE MORRISSETTE

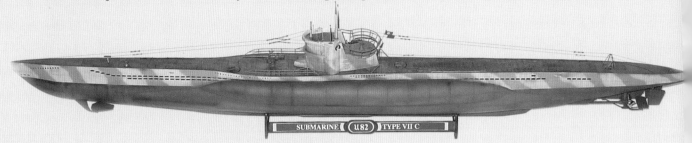

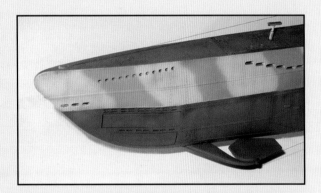

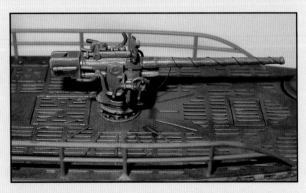

9th FLOTILLA TYPE VIIC   1/40 scale   Dave Goddard

After well over thirty years spent building AFV and aircraft models, Dave Goddard ventured into the world of radio-controlled model submarines, and this is the very convincing result. The model is based on the Robbe kit, but it has been considerably refined over time with the addition of various kit parts and scratchbuilt fittings and is, moreover, a continuing project as he is constantly modifying it!

The conning tower, for example, has been replaced with an item from the Accurate Armour range—not quite in scale, but close enough—and deck fittings and the 8.8cm deck gun come from the same source. The deck rail is scratchbuilt using brass rod, whilst the figures are from the Andrea Miniatures range. All the free-flooding holes were carefully drilled out and the torpedo doors were scribed into the hull mouldings.

The model had been repainted several times over the years, weathered sparingly with a product that creates genuine rust.

Dave's model is a dynamic diver rather than a static diver, so it has a rather low waterline and needs to work up some speed before it can submerge. The kit motors were replaced with a unit from Ships 'n' Things, geared at a ratio of 3:1 ratio rather than using direct drive to the propellers, and the batteries have been replaced with two 7.2V units. Dave's model can run for about 40–50 minutes, depending upon how many times it is dived. The bow planes work via a hook-up above the wtc (watertight cylinder) and into the rear of that unit.

Inspired by an unusual wartime photograph (reproduced at right) in a book on submarines, Mario Grima, from Pennsylvania, set about recreating one of a batch of submarines under construction, gradually rusting and festooned with scaffolding, and camouflaged to keep out the prying eyes of Allied aircraft in the latter stages of the war.

The model is based on the Revell kit of *U 99* but of course bears little resemblance to the end product that the kit manufacturer intended. It was first built up internally with a pressure hull and bulkheads, the former made from a simple ABS pipe and the latter using Plastruct 'I' and corner-beam plastic strip. The oval conning tower was made from a drop tank out of an aircraft kit, which proved to be the perfect size and shape. Most of the detail parts scattered over the U-boat and diorama came from assorted kit spare parts or model railway accessories, although many were scratchbuilt. In order to create an atmosphere of authenticity, real rust powder was used in the final coating of the boat and metallic structures.

COURTESY MARIO GRIMA

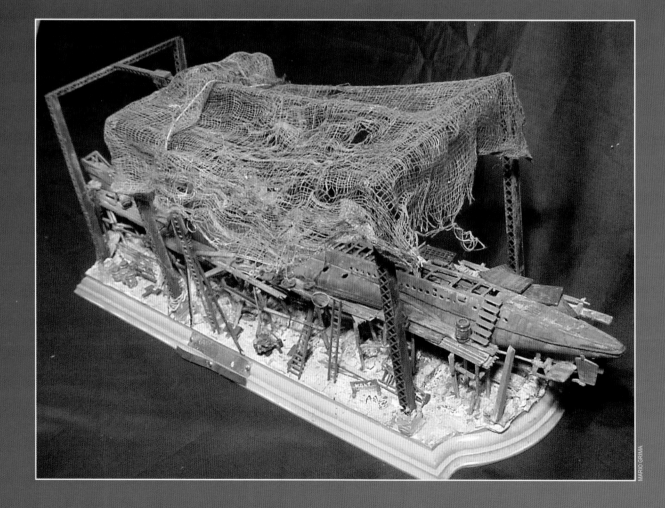

MARIO GRIMA

MARIO GRIMA

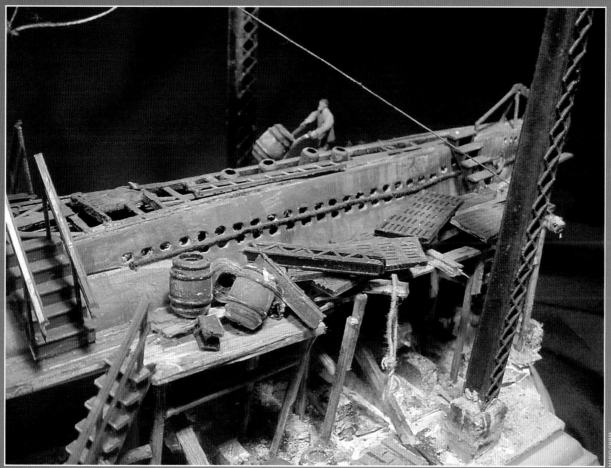

MARIO GRIMA

A phenomenal amount of work went into Mario's unique model, as these photographs show. Each angle shows something different and surprising. Mario is well-known as a builder of model submarines, to a variety of scales and nationalities, and from all eras. His recent projects have included the CSS *Hunley* in 1/72 scale, a huge, 1/32 scale working model of the USS *Ling* and a 1/48 scale model of the Japanese submarine *I-29*.

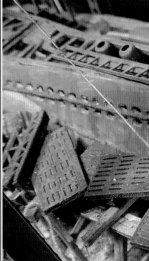

ALL PHOTOS: MARIO GRIMA

U 99 1/125 scale Ingemar Caisander

This Type VIIB model was built essentially straight out of the Revell box with some added detailing. It benefits from having the 200-plus free-flooding vents opened up, with a simulated pressure hull within to prevent 'see-through' in the midships section, the diesel intakes opened up and mesh guards added, some thinning of the net cutters at the bow and the replacement of all guard rail with copper wire for a more true-to-scale appearance.

The propeller shaft assembly called for a lot of patience (and some quick drying glue!) as it proved rather flimsy and difficult to align. The shafts were replaced with steel rod.

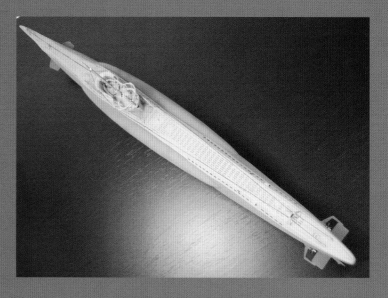

Views of Ingemar's completed model. It makes for an interesting comparison with the 1/125 scale Revell model of Prien's *U 47* (see page 48), with which it shares some common mouldings. The paint used to finish the model is Humbrol 79 (lower hull) and 145 (upper hull and conning tower).

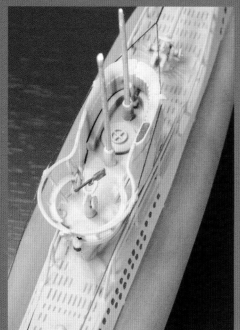

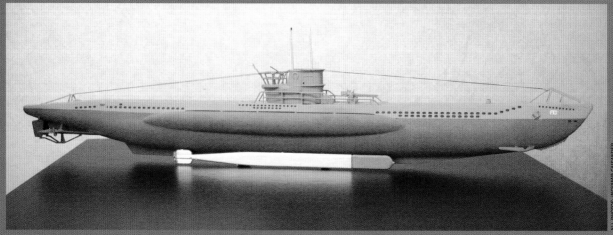

Type VIIC 1/72 scale Simon Mercs

Simon Mercs runs a small model production studio in Florida, and this model, produced for one of his clients and to the latter's specifications, is based on the Amati kit, a multimedia product with components in resin, wood, cast metal, laser-etched brass and plastic and a full-size set of profile and plan drawings.

This particular model, says Simon, was a challenge, giving the builder a feel for scratchbuilding whilst providing the insurance of 'safety' that a kit provides. Multimedia kits call for multimedia adhesives, and both epoxy resin and cyano-acrylate ('super glue')—with an accelerator when fixing wood to metal—were required for this model. Levels had to be constantly checked throughout the assembly process and bonding allowed to take place under pressure to ensure strength of adhesion. Moreover, all surfaces needed to be carefully primed before the finishing coats could be applied. Deck gun and rail were applied last, after all basic painting had been completed, owing to their fragility.

The kit proved to be a good one in terms of accuracy of fit, and modelling putty was used only sparingly.

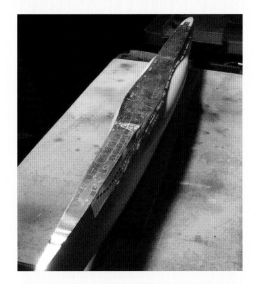

These photographs illustrate various stages in the construction of the model, and show the hefty resin hull and the excellent brass-etched decking supplied with the Amati kit, and steps in the painting of the model. This is not a kit to be spliced together in one evening!

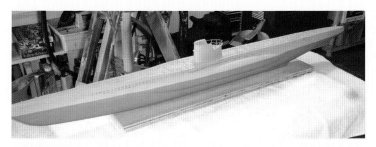

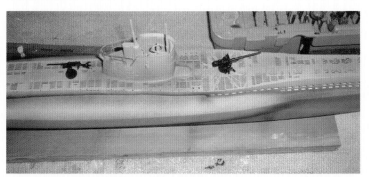

Simon's model has been painted in Dark Gull Grey and Gunship Grey, with 'rust' and 'diesel' airbrush effects, the paint scheme having been taken from the prop used in the film *Das Boot*, as per his client's request. The model—shown completed at left, with decals in place—measures 37 inches in overall length and is highly detailed. Further examples of Simon's work can be seen at www.thekitfactory.com.

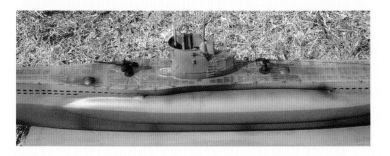

ALL PHOTOS: SIMON MERCS

Schemes

U 83 (Type VIIB)   July 1942   ▶

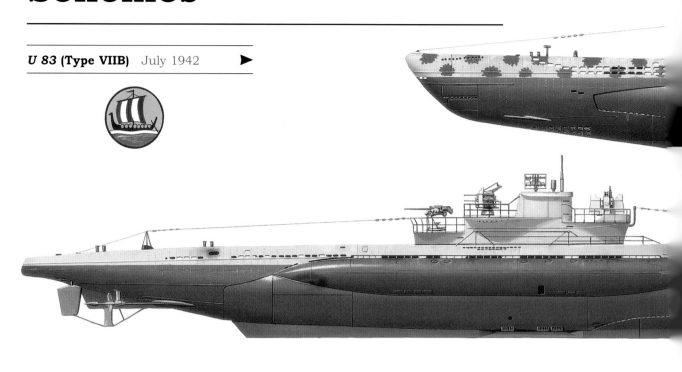

U 453 (Type VIIC)   ▶

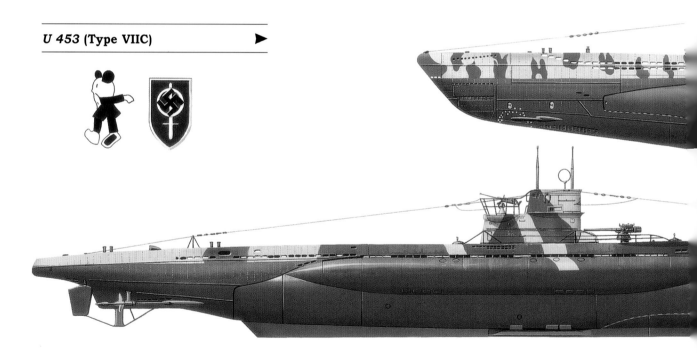

U 707 (Type VIIC)   1943   ▶

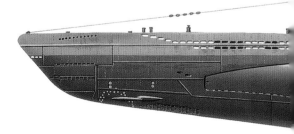

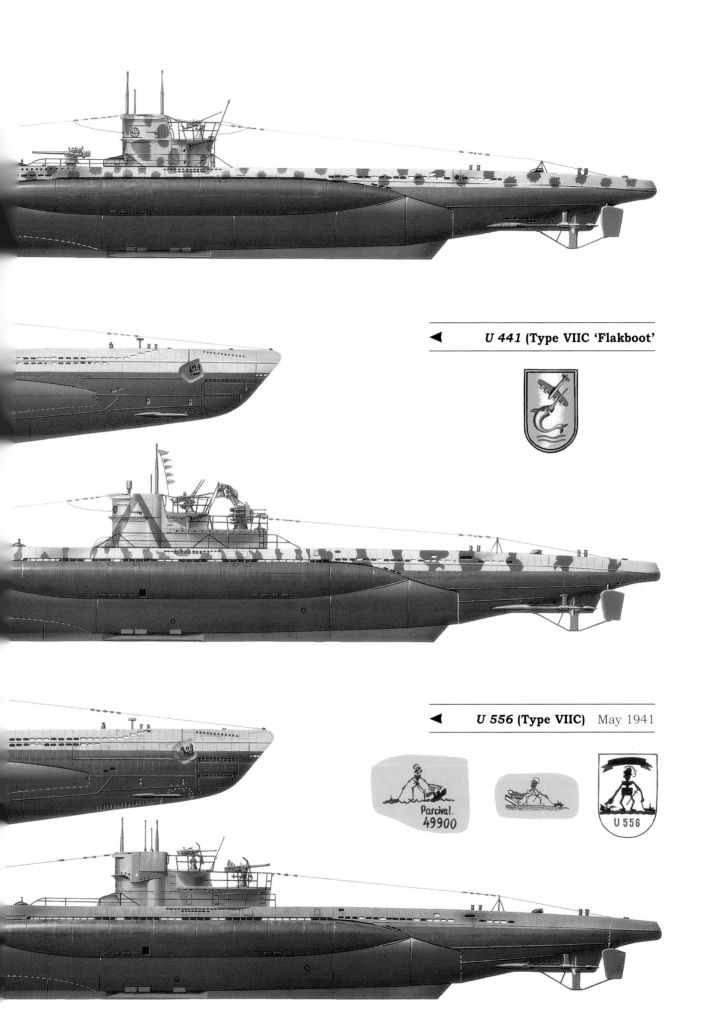

◀ *U 441* (Type VIIC 'Flakboot'

◀ *U 556* (Type VIIC) May 1941

Parcival.
49900

U 556

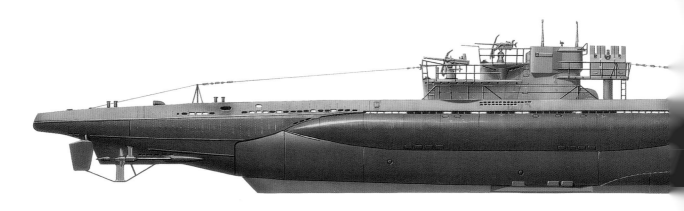

U 338 insignia

U 201 (Type VIIC) 1942 ▶

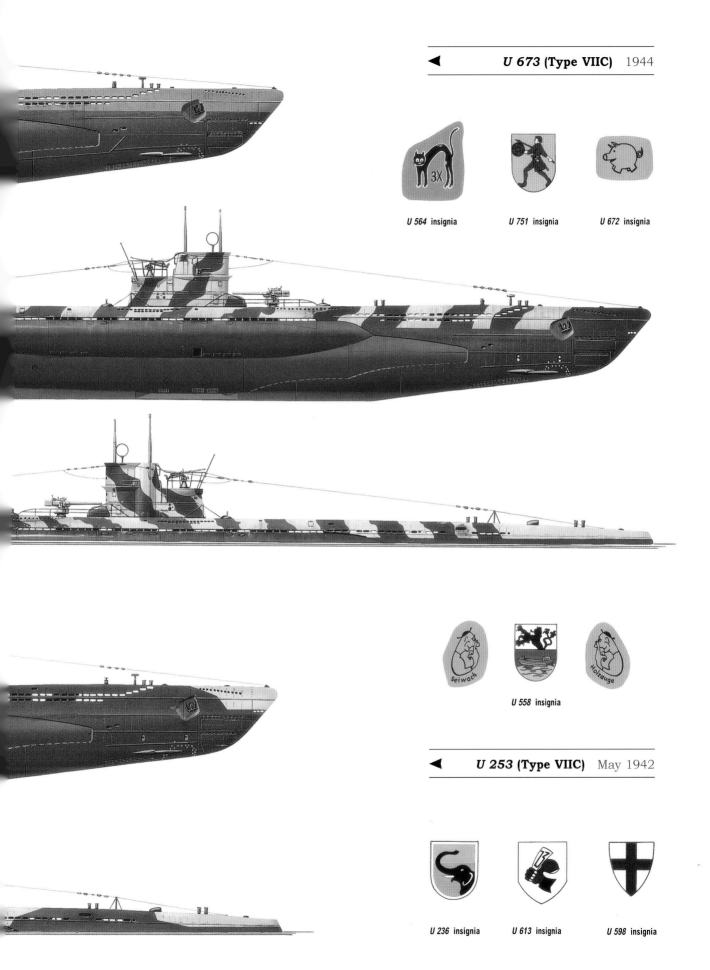

U 564 insignia

U 751 insignia

U 672 insignia

U 558 insignia

◄　***U 253* (Type VIIC)**　May 1942

U 236 insignia

U 613 insignia

U 598 insignia

U 564 CONNING TOWER 1/32 scale Ian Ruscoe

Ian Ruscoe is one of the outstanding contemporary ship modellers, and his excellent model of a Type VIIC conning tower is built from the Andrea Miniatures kit, which is supplied as resin, white-metal and etched-brass components and has 'rub-down' decals for *U 564*, a 7.Flottille or a 9.Flottille boat.

Intricately detailed models such as this one are best built up as a series of sub-assemblies, each completed and painted prior to being added to the model. The whole is set in a 'sea' fashioned from Interior Polyfilla on a suitable rigid base, sculpted whilst wet and, when dry, sprayed and varnished.

The general overhead view of the model shows the clean, sharp detailing provided by the resin and etched brass components of the Andrea Miniatures kit. The Kriegsmarine ensign and victory pennants are provided in the kit as paper designs.

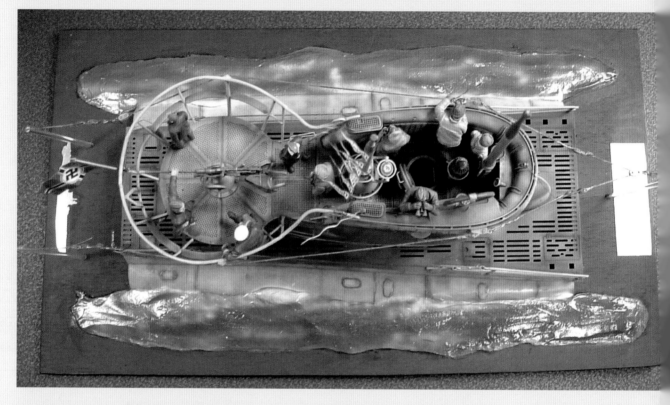

Closer to the model, one can appreciate the skilled workmanship that has gone into it, with painstaking shading and weathering adding to the overall authenticity of the piece. Not all the figures seen here are provided in the kit: Andrea Miniatures provide excellent white-metal castings for some, but four extra crew members are present on the model, drawn from the Wolf, Hornet and Accurate Armour ranges. All are finished using artists' oils, following the careful application of primer.

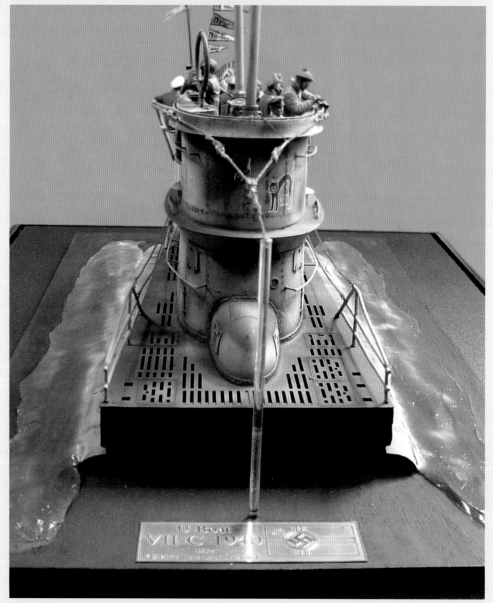

Further photographs of the Andrea Miniatures conning tower model, these views highlighting the excellent painting work on the figures. Readers of the second volume in the *ShipCraft* series will recall Ian's outstanding dioramic model of HMS *Prince of Wales* at Singapore—one-tenth the scale but no less dramatic for that.

U 47 1/125 scale Ingemar Caisander

Like the *U 99* shown on page 38, this demonstration model has been built up from the Revell kit with little modification, and, although it captures the characteristics of the Type VIIB, the interior detailing, says Ingemar, leaves a lot to be desired. For example, the bow and after torpedo tubes are far too short, while the absence of any portrayal of the pressure hull is a serious omission.

The whole interior will need extensive scratch-building to look even remotely like the real thing. The parts depicting the diesel engines are very simplified, with the electric motors simply bolted on: they will have to be separated, extensively detailed and rearranged into their correct compartments. Clutches for the propeller shafts would need to be added as well.

As before, the kit benefits from having the propeller shafts replaced and the guard rail etc supplanted by steel rod and copper wire, respectively. As Ingemar points out, the interior detailing is not only sparse but frequently inaccurate, although it does give an indication of the general layout of the Type VII. The kit is these days also showing its age, with some warping of the hull halves evident and the fit of the parts not always tight.

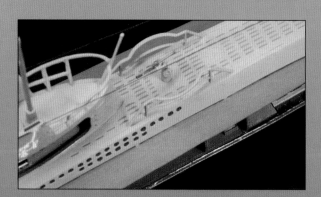

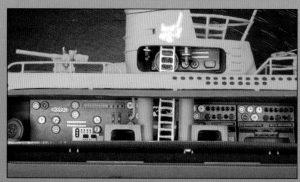

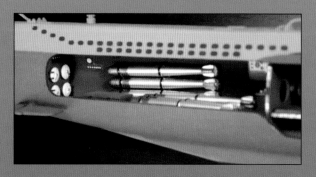

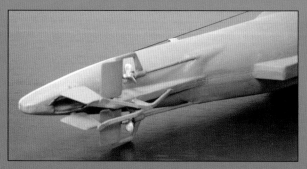

Appearance

AMONGST all the versions of the Type VII U-boat, it is hardly surprising that the VIIC, since it accounted for the vast bulk of the production effort, was the model that saw numerous variations in configuration, particularly with respect to its gun armament: the submarine technology of the day was such that the U-boat had to spend most of its time on the surface, open to the threat from aircraft. Early in the war the central Atlantic was free from hostile aircraft, but with the advent of escort aircraft carriers and very-long-range bombers the gap was gradually plugged and nowhere could a U-boat commander feel entirely safe—even at night.

If a submarine were unable to dive quickly enough to avoid a sudden air attack (or for any other reason), then it made sense to give it both 'eyes' and 'teeth' to enable it to cope more readily, and, in essence, these are what Atlantic U-boats received from about mid-1943 onwards.

'EYES'

'Eyes'—radar—in fact came to Type VII U-boats quite late on, as it was not until 1942 that any such equipment was installed. This equipment fell into one of two categories—passive radar, for the detection of signals transmitted by enemy aircraft or ships; and active radar, for locating enemy aircraft or ships by deliberately transmitting signals (with the obvious potential for self-betrayal). The two categories of equipment were distinguished in Kriegsmarine service by their prefixes: FuMB (Funkmeß-Beobachtungsgerät, or radar observation apparatus—i.e., receivers) and FuMO (Funkmeßortungsgerät, or radar detection apparatus, *Ortung* meaning 'locating' or 'fixing'), respectively. It should be borne on mind that the FuMB/FuMO designations referred to the apparatus; the antenna for each

system was usually consistent, but not invariably so.

The first passive system, designed to give warning of RAF aircraft now attacking by night with the aid of the 'Leigh Light', was a primitive affair using a 'Metox' receiver with a crude antenna which was rotated manually, known officially as FuMB 1 but universally dubbed 'Biskayakreuz' (Biscay Cross). From that point on the German U-Boat Service played 'catch-up' as the British

Left: The earliest detection equipment fitted aboard operational Type VII U-boats was the so-called 'Biskaya-kreuz', seen here projecting vertically from the conning tower of an unidentified U-boat. Made of wood and cheap to manufacture and install, it was effective for about six months following its introduction in summer 1942, after which improved Allied radar systems rendered it obsolete.

Left: An unshielded FuMB 29 array in a Type VIIC. Like FuMB 1, this was a passive set (i.e., it did not actively emit radiation which could be detected by enemy antennae). Clearly, its fixed nature limited its search arc to roughly 30 degrees to port and starboard of dead forward; a full scan required the boat herself to be turned.

progressively introduced more advanced airborne detection equipment and the Kriegsmarine attempted to foil it—although, it has to be said, Naval High Command did not entirely embrace the technology, unappreciative, perhaps, of the advantages that it offered.

The FuMB 29 incorporated a fixed array ('Bali'), installed on the forward contours of the conning tower (and generally covered by a shield) and therefore requiring the boat itself to be circled if all-round search was called for. A 'Naxos' receiver system, and a version of the widely used 'Seetakt', FuMB 29 was introduced late in 1942 after the Germans had begin to suffer appalling losses of U-boats to air attack and had discovered, belatedly, that the principal reason was that British ASW aircraft were employing microwave radar. It often also featured the 'Palau' butterfly-shaped direction-finding antenna. The following year saw a number of Type VIIs fitted with FuMB 7, another 'Naxos' set but with a distinctive retractable antenna.

This set was succeeded by the FuMO 30, characterised by a 1.4 × 1m rectangular antenna in a turntable fitted to a housing on the side of the conning tower. Though an improvement on the FuMO 29, it was not entirely satisfactory. A few Type VIIs were equipped with it from about mid-1944.

The most advanced radar fitting in Type VIIs was the FuMO 61 ('Hohentweil-U'), based on the FuMG (Funk-

Left: The antenna for the FuMO 30 active radar system, the angular housing on the port side of the conning tower permitting its retraction. The butterfly-shaped devices are the 'Palau' direction-finders.

Above: Three Type VIICs (and, far left, a Type IXD) after their surrender at Wilhelmshaven, with late-war modifications in evidence.
Below: Two views of the 8.8cm deck gun. To save weight, and because it was increasingly little used, this weapon was removed from most Type VIIs as the war progressed.

meßgerät) 200 equipment used successfully by the Luftwaffe. Like the preceding systems, it used a 1.4 × 1m antenna.

Installing radar systems was never a high priority in the U-Boat Service: commanders did not in general lobby for them, suspicious that their use might betray the presence of their boats to prying aircraft, and there was the perennial problem of interference from sea water (damage, corrosion, etc. to the antennae). Moreover, the boats' low pro-

file and their relative unsteadiness placed severe limits on the usefulness of the equipment in anything other than a flat calm.

'TEETH'

By far the most significant changes concerning the Type VII's outward appearance were the progressive upgradings of anti-aircraft weaponry. In addition to its 8.8cm deck gun, the Type VII generally mounted a single 2cm C/30, aft of

the conning tower on the deck. The Type VIIB saw the gun moved up on to a platform on the after conning tower itself, where it could command far better sky arcs.

From late 1941/early 1942 a series of modifications to the AA armament began to be introduced into the U-boat fleet in response to the growing vulnerability of the boats to air attack: these changes were many and varied, but showed a tendency to increase the number of barrels as the war ground on. There were a number of 'official' configurations, for which the conning towers were extended; but there were also some unofficial layouts, approved by individual commanders if not by higher authority. It is possible to identify four standard fits—three for the VIIC and one for the VIID—in addition to that with which the early boats were first commissioned (surviving Type VIIs and VIIBs were also upgraded as appropriate):

1. From late 1942 some boats had their conning tower platform widened in order to accommodate an air raid shelter (a small metal cupboard) and a housing for the radar antenna, and a pair of Breda twin 13.2mm machine guns in addition to the 2cm was frequently fitted;

2. At about the same time a lower 'Wintergarten' was introduced on other boats—a longitudinal aftward extension of the conning-tower structure forming a second, lower AA platform and carrying a second 2cm mounting. Some boats (particularly those used for training) had single 2cms still; others (generally the operational boats) were fitted with twins.

3. On the Type VIIDs, the presence of the mine chutes abaft the conning tower precluded the addition of a 'Wintergarten' and hence the gun platform was widened to take a pair of 2cm mountings side by side.

4. During the last year of the war many Type VIICs were seen with an AA fit of two twin (or occasionally single) 2cm on the upper platform and a single 3.7cm M 42U on the lower.

Other permutations applied to individual boats and included the addition of 20mm MG 151s in various locations; some extempory (and largely unsuccessful) fits involved an additional platform forward of the conning tower (the 8.8cm was unshipped from very many boats, both to save weight and because it was increasingly rarely employed) and the carrying of 2cm quadruple mountings—indeed, four VIICs (*U 256*, *U 441*,

Above left: The conning tower of U 255, seen here in 1943, with weatherbeaten paintwork and machine guns evident. Just detectable, right, is the boat's FuMB 7 'Naxos' antenna.

Above right: A common 'Wintergarten' arrangement on a late-war Type VIIC (U 1168)—a twin 3.7cm with, higher and forward, a twin 2cm.

Below: Detail of one of the four Type VIIs converted to 'Flakboote', in this instance U 441. The FuMO 30 antenna is clearly visible.

Right: Type VIIC conning
tower physiognomy.

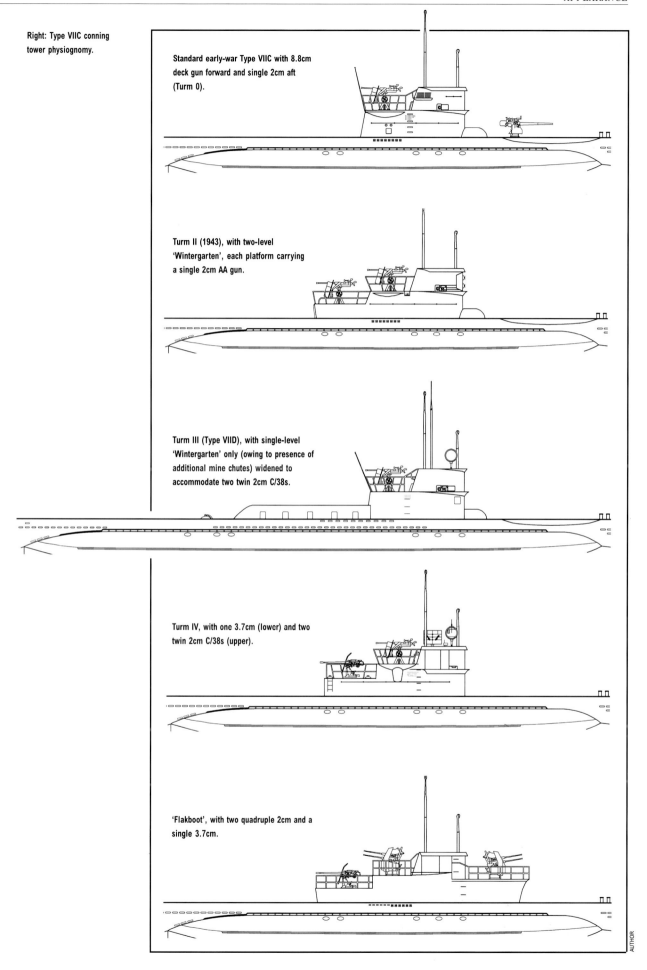

Standard early-war Type VIIC with 8.8cm
deck gun forward and single 2cm aft
(Turm 0).

Turm II (1943), with two-level
'Wintergarten', each platform carrying
a single 2cm AA gun.

Turm III (Type VIID), with single-level
'Wintergarten' only (owing to presence of
additional mine chutes) widened to
accommodate two twin 2cm C/38s.

Turm IV, with one 3.7cm (lower) and two
twin 2cm C/38s (upper).

'Flakboot', with two quadruple 2cm and a
single 3.7cm.

AUTHOR

COURTESY DAG PUBLICATIONS

U 621 and *U 953*) were temporarily converted to 'Flakboote', equipped with a single 3.7cm and two quadruple 2cm mountings.

These rather desperate measures notwithstanding, the increased AA armament did little to improve the U-boats' survival rate, and once the Allied ASW pilots got wind of the possibility of being met with a hail of shell rather than a spurt they modified their approach tactics accordingly. It made little difference: a surfaced U-boat, whether slow-moving or stationary, was still more or less a sitting duck, bristling with barrels or not. Over 200 U-boats of all types—a quarter of the total number to see service—were sunk by air attack during the war.

COLOUR SCHEMES

Warship colour schemes are frequently a contentious issue, and those used by the Kriegsmarine are as contentious as any. There is much agreement concerning the schemes worn by U-boats, but there is also a good deal of doubt, particularly with regard to those boats which carried disruptive camouflage. However, making judgements from wartime photographs is less hazardous than is generally the case with other types of vessels, while from the modelmaker's point of view there is a good deal of latitude available in choosing how best to portray the appropriate paintwork for his creation.

AUTHOR'S COLLECTION

AUTHOR'S COLLECTION

Above: A photograph believed to be of the VIIC/41 *U 977* at La Plata, showing an AA arrangement of two twin 2cm and a single 3.7cm (Turm IV). Left: A similar arrangement, but with a shielded 2cm Flakvierling in place of the lower 3.7cm.

Left: The after quadruple 2cm mounting aboard the 'Flakboot' *U 441*.

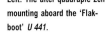

AUTHOR'S COLLECTION

Above: An unidentified Type VIIC finished in Hellgrau 50 and with Schiffsbodenfarbe III Grau applied to the lower hull. Very unusually, the forward face of the conning tower seems also to carry the latter colour.

Below: A military band strikes up aboard a Type VIIB. The boat's pale grey paintwork extends over the uppersurfaces of the saddle tanks.

COURTESY LAWRENCE PATERSON

His task is eased because, perhaps without exception, all uncamouflaged Type VII U-boats were finished in shades of grey (to include, on occasion, black and white), which makes the interpretation of contemporary black-and-white images a little less fraught than had other principal colours been involved. Furthermore, the U-boats' unique environment—if a boat was not actually beneath the waves, then it was regularly swamped by them— resulted in a heavy toll on paintwork being taken by the ele-

ments of wind and water, which means that pristine finishes were short-lived and that the original colouring quickly became 'weathered'. Even more latitude is offered for other reasons. Towards the end of the war, for example, paint stocks were in short supply, and rarely can it be categorically stated that a particular boat carried the 'official' colours. The influence of the commanders also came into play, especially if a boat were on a long patrol: first, many of them authorised individual paint schemes, whether in the process of a 'clean up' or perhaps on a whim; secondly, the smart appearance of his boat would likely be towards the bottom of his list of priorities, or absent from it altogether, and so the deterioration of the paintwork may well have been left unattended. All that said, there are some generalities that can be observed.

Most early Type VIIs were delivered from the shipyard with the hull, conning tower and main deck gun in matt Hellgrau 50 (light grey; not identical in shade to the Luftwaffe's Hellgrau 76). This paint continued in use throughout the war but one of two other, darker shades is known to have been applied to very many boats—Dunkelgrau 51 (dark bluish grey) and Schlickgrau 58 (literally, 'mud grey'). Blaugrau 58.1 (blue-grey) and Blauschwarz 58.2 (blue-black) are also thought to have been used on some boats. Beneath the waterline, Schiffsbodenfarbe III Grau (literally,

55

Plans

Original builder's plans for Type VIIC, F. Schichau GmbH, Danzig

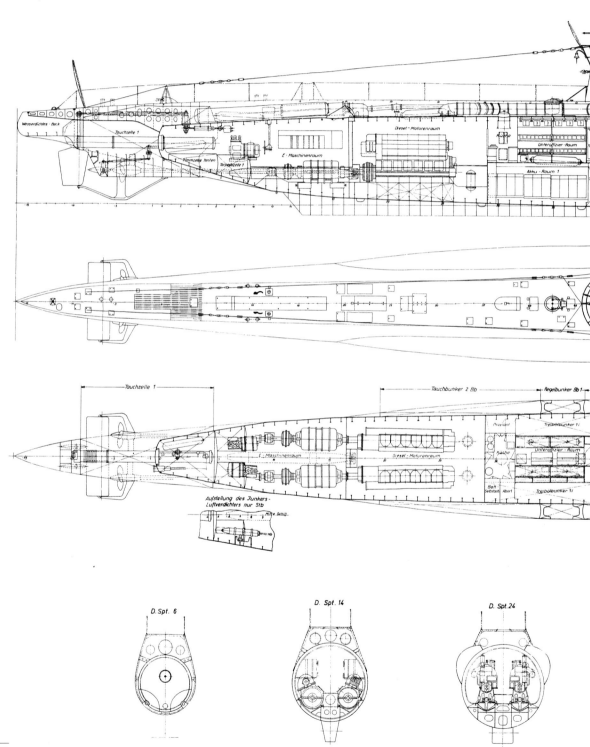

1/200 scale

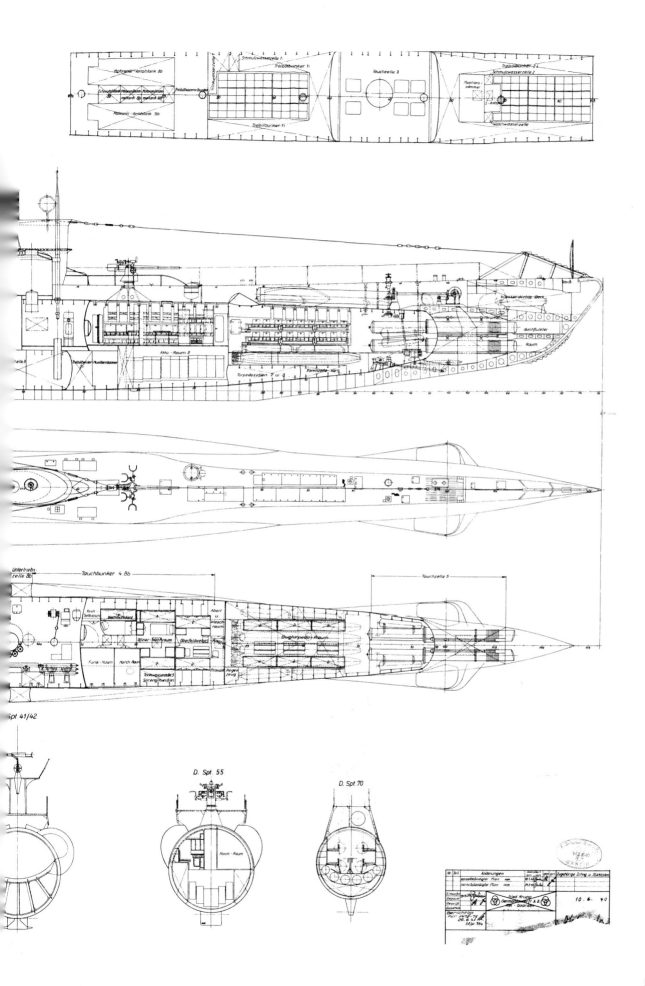

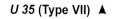

U 35 (Type VII) ▲   *U 237* (Type VIIC) ▼

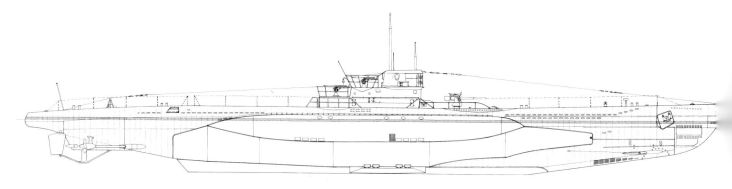

1/350 scale

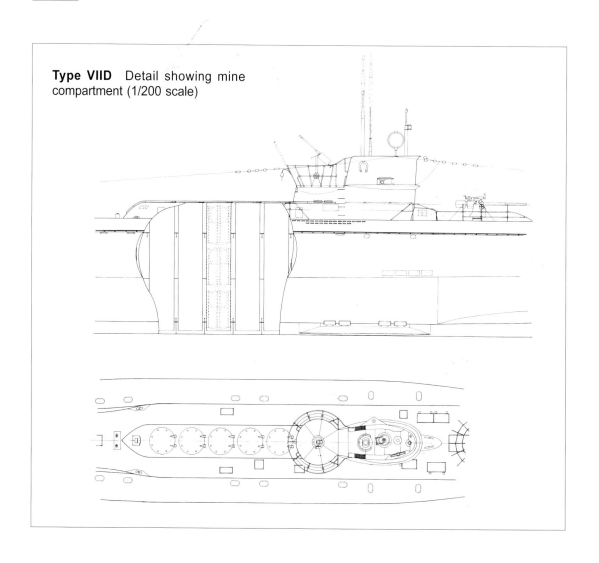

Type VIID Detail showing mine
compartment (1/200 scale)

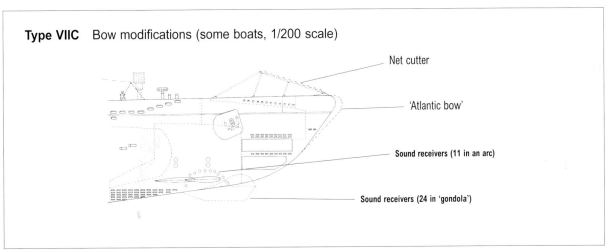

Type VIIC Bow modifications (some boats, 1/200 scale)

Net cutter

'Atlantic bow'

Sound receivers (11 in an arc)

Sound receivers (24 in 'gondola')

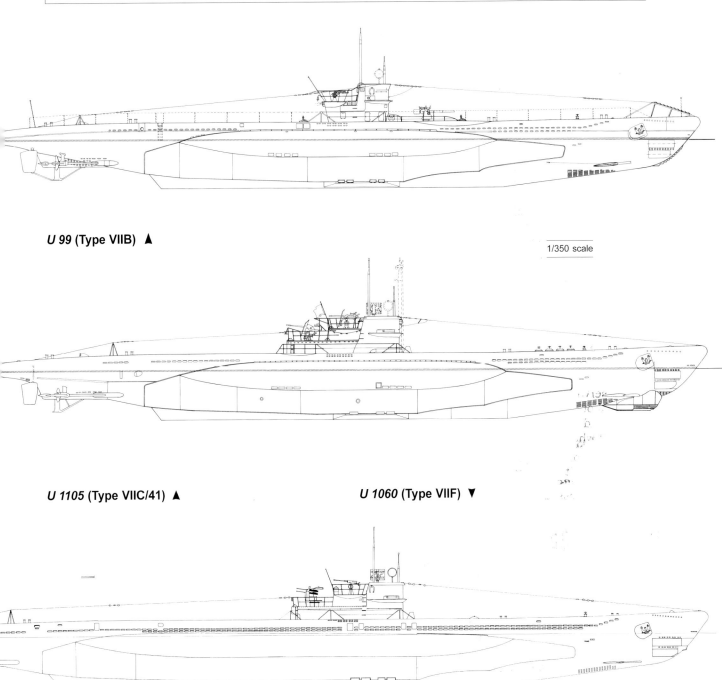

U 99 (Type VIIB) ▲

1/350 scale

U 1105 (Type VIIC/41) ▲   *U 1060* (Type VIIF) ▼

Left: Some U-boats received an unofficial disruptive camouflage, although its effectiveness was arguable. This is *U 82*.

'ship's ground colour grey') was used as an anti-fouling finish. The wooden decking was generally coated in a blackish preservative, but of course in service this quickly became scuffed, worn, stained and weathered; and there was certainly no desire for holystoning in the wartime U-Boat Service.

The consensus of opinion seems to be that those boats painted in disruptive camouflage used either Schlickgrau or Dunkelgrau to break up the underlying Hellgrau. However, there is a possibility that dark green was used in some instances, whilst some Mediterranean U-boats are said to have used Blu Scuro (dark blue—an Italian-manufactured paint) over the Hellgrau base.

There were, for certain, plenty of variations and exceptions to these general observations. It is unwise to be dogmatic about the colour schemes of U-boats, and one should always be wary of those who are.

INDIVIDUAL MARKINGS

In small, close-knit military communities the spirit of friendship, 'togetherness' and camaraderie was (and is) frequently expressed in illustrative form on some external part of a crew's weaponry, not always officially sanctioned but usually permitted, if only as a means of holding up morale. The U-Boat Service was alive with such graphics, many well known and well-documented and many, no doubt, about which nothing is known because the boats and their crews either went unphotographed or were lost at sea.

Left: One of the most famous U-boat insignia was Prien's 'Bull of Scapa Flow', seen here applied to his *U 47*.

Left: Prien's 'snorting bull' insignia, in various forms, was later adopted by the Kriegsmarine's 7.U-Flottille (7th Submarine Flotilla)

Right: Kapitänleutnant Erich Topp's *U 552* bearing a red 'devil' silhouette on the conning tower (handed, to starboard also). The 7.U-Flottille's bull insignia is also present, further aft.

Right: Swastikas were not commonly seen on U-boats, but Type VIIC *U 132* displayed one on her conning tower, superimposed on the German eagle.

Far right: *U 564*'s conning tower, showing the black cat insignia of Korvettenkapitän Reinhard Suhren's boat.

Right: The laughing sawfish identified boats of 9.U-Flottille. This is *U 821*, a Type VIIC , at Brest in June 1944, with the insignia curving around the fairing for the radar antenna.

Far right: The Type VIIC *U 407* of the same flotilla, with the coat of arms of Danzig (now renamed Gdansk) on the forward contour.

61

U 995

The Last of the Many

OF THE SEVEN hundred or so Type VII U-boats built, only one complete example exists today (although over sixty were scuttled after the war and may in time yield a restoration project). *U 995*, a type VIIC/41, was built by Blohm und Voss and commissioned in September 1943; during her wartime career she sank four Allied ships. Along with the rest of the U-boat fleet, she was surrendered in 1945 and some years later was commissioned into the Royal Norwegian Navy and named *Kaura*. In the late 1960s the boat was stricken by the Norwegians but was returned to Germany, restored and put on public display at Laboe, near Kiel, where she is today administered as a museum boat.

CARSTEN HEINTZE

GERHARD KOOP

Selected References

BOOKS

Bagnasco, Ermino, *Submarines of World War II*, Arms & Armour Press (London, 1977)

Blair, Clay, *Hitler's U-Boat War*, 2 vols, Random House (New York, 1996, 2000)

Breyer, Siegfried, and Koop, Gerhard, *The German Navy at War. Vol. 2: The U-Boat*, Schiffer Publishing (Atglen, 1991)

Buchheim, Lothar-Günther, *The Boat*, Collins (London, 1974)

Chesneau, Roger (ed.), *Conway's All the World's Fighting Ships, 1922–1946*, Conway Maritime Press (London, 1980)

Dönitz, Karl, *Ten Years and Twenty Days*, Weidenfeld & Nicolson (London, 1959)

Heintze, Carsten, *U-Boote: Modelle und Ihre Vorbilder*, Verlag für Technik und Handwerk (Baden-Baden, 2003)

Högel, Georg, *U-Boat Emblems of World War II, 1939–1945*, Schiffer Publishing (Atglen, 1999)

Köhl, Fritz, and Niestlé, Axel, *Vom Original zum Modell: Uboottyp VII C*, Bernard & Graefe Verlag (Bonn, 1997)

Lenton, H. T., *German Submarines*, 2 vols, Macdonald (London, 1965)

Mallmann Showell, Jak P., *Enigma U-Boats: Breaking the Code—the True Story*, Ian Allan (Hersham, 2002)

Martin, Rodney J., *Silent Runner: Wolfgang Heyda, U-Boat Commander*, privately published (2003)

Miller, David, *U-Boats: History, Development and Equipment, 1914–1945*, Conway Maritime Press (London, 2000)

Nowarra, Heinz J., *German U-Boat Type VII: Grey Wolves of the Sea*, Schiffer Publishing (Atglen, 1992)

Paterson, Lawrence, *U-Boat War Patrol: The Hidden Photographic Diary of U564*, Greenhill Books (London, 2004)

Price, Alfred, *Aircraft versus Submarine*, William Kimber (London, 1973)

Rohwer, J., and Hümmelchen, G., *Chronology of the War at Sea: The Naval History of World War Two*, Greenhill Books (London, 1992)

Roskill, Capt S. W., *The War at Sea* (3 vols), HMSO (London, 1954–61)

Rössler, Eberhard, *The U-Boat: The Evolution and Technical History of German Submarines*, Arms & Armour Press (London, 1981)

Stern, Robert C., *U-Boats in Action*, Squadron/Signal Publications (Warren, 1977)

Westwood, David, *The Type VII U-Boat* ('Anatomy of the Ship' series), Conway Maritime Press (London, 1984)

Werner, Herbert A., *Iron Coffins: A Personal Account of the German U-Boat Battles of World War II*, Da Capo Press (2002)

Wiper, Steve, *Type VII U-Boats* ('Warship Pictorial' series), Classic Warships Publishing (Tucson, 2004)

PLANS

Köhl, Fritz, and Niestlé, Axel, *Planmappe: Uboottyp VII C*, Bernard & Graefe Verlag (Bonn, 2003)

WEBSITES (Specialist)

http://uboat.net — One of the internet's best overall sources of information concerning U-boats.

http://www.uboatnet.de — Another excellent site, in German; not to be confused with the foregoing.

http://www.german-navy.de/kriegsmarine/ships/uboats— Very good general site about the German Navy since World War I.

http://www.subcommittee.com/— Superb general site about submarines.

http://www.uboatwar.net — First-rate site maintained by Lawrence Paterson.

http://www.u47.org — Comprehensive site about Prien's famous boat.

WEBSITES (General/modelling)

http://www.steelnavy.com
http://www.modelwarships.com
http://www.ipmsusa.org
http://www.warshipmodelsunderway.com
http://www.smmlonline.com